Collins

AF662434

Enhanced

Science Now

A Science Textbook based on Holistic Learning Theory

3

Name : ....

Grade : .... Section : ....

I live in water. When I'm hungry, I do something cool. My tummy stretches out to hug my food outside my body. It magically turns into a yummy treat. Then, I slurp it back in, happy and full. It's like a taste adventure under the sea! What am I? ....

Series Editor | Jyothsna Natraj

HarperCollinsPublishers

Publishing operations in 17 countries and 120+ imprints globally

William Collins' dream of knowledge for all began with the publication of his first book in 1819. A self-educated mill worker, he not only enriched millions of lives, but also founded a flourishing publishing house. Today, staying true to this spirit, Collins books are packed with inspiration, innovation and practical expertise. They place you at the centre of a world of possibility and give you exactly what you need to explore it.

Published by Collins Learning
An imprint of HarperCollins*Publishers* India
Building No. 10, Tower A, 4th Floor, DLF Cyber City, Gurugram, Haryana 122002, India

First edition: 2024
Reprint edition: 2025
ISBN: 978-93-6213-154-6

Content developed by **Excelsoft Technologies Pvt Ltd.**
Artwork, typesetting and layout by **AptaraCorp Ltd., Mammoth Studioz Ltd, iBook Services**
Printed and bound in India by Saurabh Printers Pvt. Ltd.

ACKNOWLEDGEMENTS

Title Page: Lelia Valduga

Inside: Page **4:** Tomas Knopp; **8:** blueringmedia; **17:** Chase Dekker Wild-Life Images, skynesher; **20:** Pakin Songmor; **26:** Photo by Bhaskar Dutta, Moncherie, R.Tsubin, Afriandi, KieselUndStein; **35:** Chaithanya Krishnan, Peter Guttman, tomodaji, Photographed by PhotostOry, JackF, retales botijero; **42:** Deven Dadbhawala; **47:** Aaron Foster, aapsky, Diane D Miller; **55:** IconicBestiary; **57:** -AZ-, GlobalP, flubydust, texcroc; **66:** ajaykampani; **77:** EllenMoran, Amer Ghazzal, David Merron Photography, SBTheGreenMan, Burazin; **96:** chuchart duangdaw; **118:** artisticco; **135:** dlewis33, Viktorcvetkovic, Visoot Uthairam, **144:** baytunc, SarapulSar38, s-cphoto, deepblue4you

Supplementary Booklet: Nikiteev_Konstantin, andegro4ka, Julia_Sudnitskaya, Olesia Kononenko, drmakkoy, Nadzeya_Dzivakova, pijama61, robuart, LuckyStep48, Ponomariova_Maria, AlionaManakova, Popmarleo, AlionaManakova, sarunyu_foto, eliflamra

Browse the complete Collins catalogue at www.collins.in.
For any queries/feedback, please write to us at SCHOOLSUPPORT@harpercollins.co.in.

Preface

We live in a rapidly changing world where a person's decision can have an impact on the environment and others. Should the learning approach remain the same? What type of learning and skills should be developed so that students can face the demands and challenges of everyday life and succeed in the 21st century? One way of achieving this would be adopting the *holistic learning theory*.

Holistic learning theory or *holistic education* implies that each person finds identity, meaning and purpose in life through connections to the community, to the natural world and to values such as compassion and peace. It strives to help learners grow in all dimensions: intellectual, emotional, social, artistic, moral, psychological, physical, aesthetic, creative, intuitive and spiritual.

Enhanced Science Now, a series of eight books for Classes 1 to 8, adheres to the guidelines of the *National Education Policy* (NEP) 2020 and adopts the *holistic learning theory*. This enhanced edition retains the focus of the original edition, where the development of lateral thinking, analytical, research and deduction skills in students were encouraged. While the strong content would help strengthen the knowledge of the core science subject, new features based on the holistic learning theory would help in the development of every student's intellectual, emotional, social, artistic and creative potentials. This enhanced edition, thus, is an attempt to provide meaningful learning and help the students become well-rounded adults, ready to face the challenges in the 21st century, and ultimately empower the students to discover their full potential as learners.

Key Features

- **Summary** Snapshot of the chapter in the form of a graphic organizer for quick revision
- **Exercise** Questions dealing with Remembering and Understanding levels of Bloom's taxonomy
- **Cognitive Corner** Section dealing with Applying, Analysing, Evaluating and Creating levels of Bloom's taxonomy and Life Skills
- **Worksheets** Pictorial exercises based on the United Nations Sustainable Development Goals
- **Skills You Need** A variety of interesting information and activities to introduce skill courses with some form of experiential learning
- **Happiness Activity Sheets** A variety of interesting activities based on life skills, self-awareness, other awareness, emotional needs and mental needs
- **Vernacular Names** List of plants and animals used in the book and their names in a few Indian regional languages
- **STEAM Activities** Engaging STEAM-based activities for the future problem solvers, critical thinkers, innovators and inventors

Four **assessment papers** and two **comprehensive assessment papers** have been given, in addition to the exercises at the end of each chapter.

The **Series Editor** for classes 1 to 5 is **Jyothsna Natraj**, a teacher at Vidya Mandir Senior Secondary School. She has been teaching science for over a decade. She has experience in web-based content development and has extensively used technologies such as 'SMART' tools in her classes.

Feedback, valuable comments and suggestions from the users are welcome.

Authors

Key Features

The key features of ***Enhanced Science Now*** are completely aligned with the **National Education Policy** (NEP) 2020, and have been designed based on the *holistic learning theory* to facilitate a holistic education. These features not only aim at the development of intellectual capabilities of the students but also aim at the development of physical capabilities, intellectual abilities, cognitive or mental abilities, emotional abilities and social skills.

Multifaceted features such as Cognitive Corner, Life Skills, Worksheet, Skills You Need, Happiness Activity Sheets and STEAM Activities would help in the holistic development of a student through interesting questions, projects and activities while providing experiential learning and fostering innovative thinking and creativity.

The series also aims at making the students aware of the **Sustainable Developments Goals (SDGs)**. The SDGs are the 17 Global Goals adopted by all United Nations Member States in 2015 to help end poverty, protect the planet and ensure peace and prosperity for all by 2030. Read more about the goals at https://www.un.org/sustainabledevelopment/

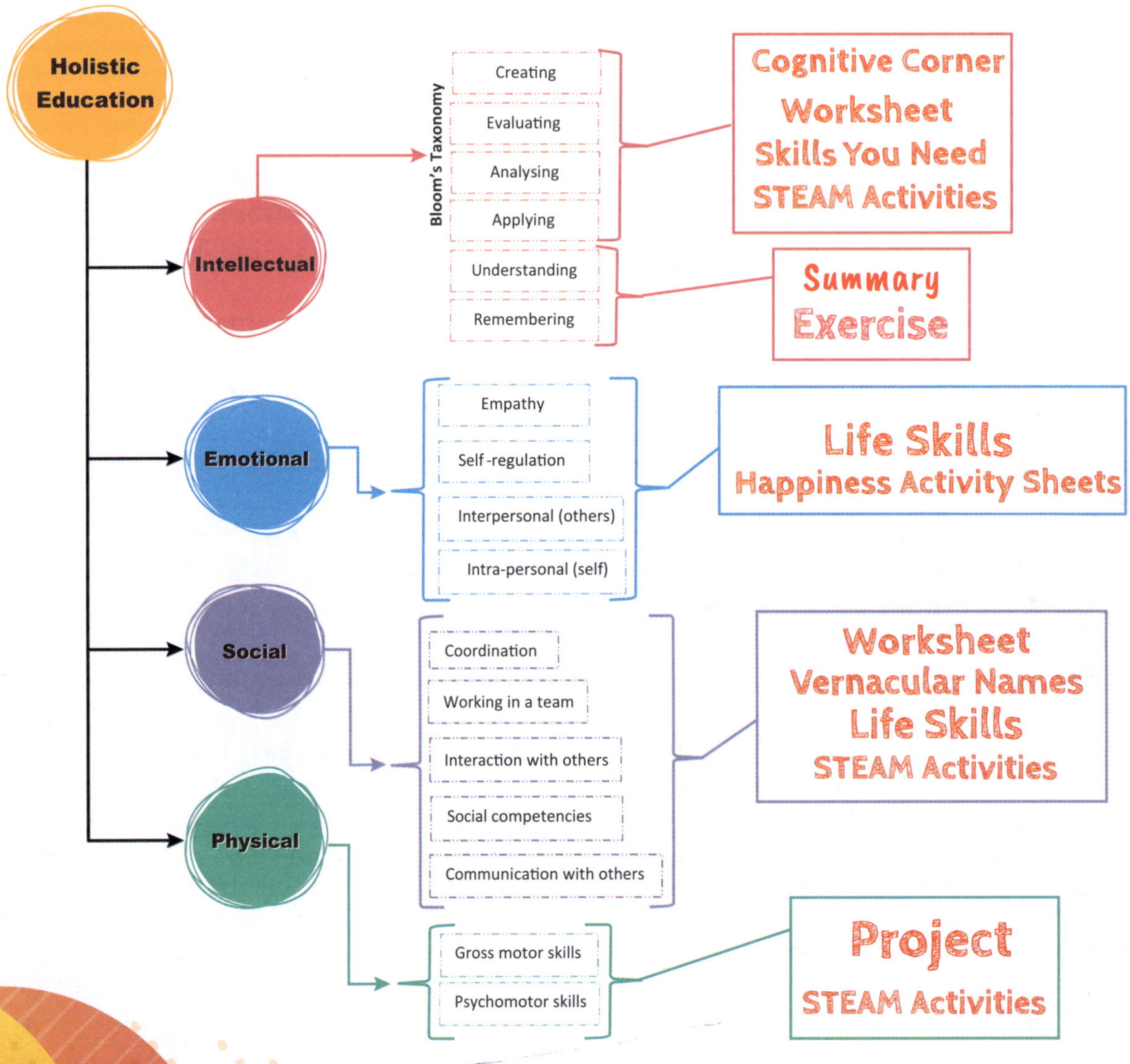

About the Features

Summary

Snapshot of the chapter in the form of a graphic organizer for quick revision

Exercise

Questions dealing with Remembering and Understanding levels of Bloom's taxonomy

Cognitive Corner

Section dealing with Applying, Analysing, Evaluating and Creating levels of Bloom's taxonomy

Critical Thinking Questions to address cognitive development such as thinking, reasoning, analysis, inference and drawing conclusions

Picture Study Questions to help develop observation and inference skills

Project Ideas for experiential learning and subject enrichment with cross-curricular links

Life Skills

Thought-provoking passage and relevant questions to help develop sensible life skills such as self-awareness, empathy and attitude towards self and others

Worksheet

Pictorial exercises at the end of each chapter based on the United Nations Sustainable Development Goals

Collins | SUSTAINABLE DEVELOPMENT GOALS

Collins Learning supports the Sustainable Development Goals

Skills You Need

A variety of interesting information and activities to introduce skill courses with some form of experiential learning

Happiness Activity Sheets

A variety of interesting activities based on life skills, self-awareness, other awareness, emotional needs and mental needs

Vernacular Names

List of plants and animals used in the book and their names in a few Indian regional languages

STEAM Activities

Engaging STEAM-based activities for the future problem solvers, critical thinkers, innovators and inventors

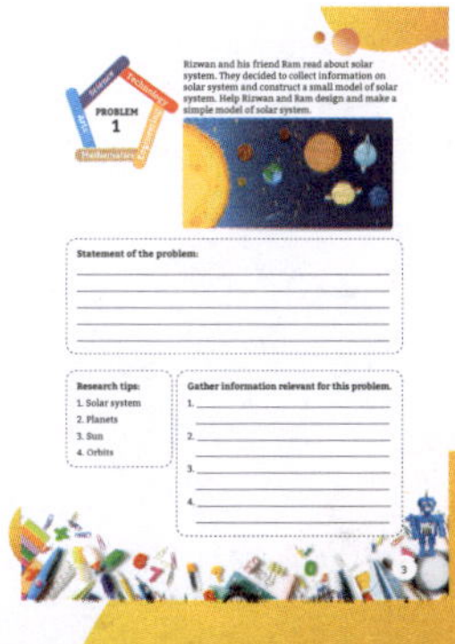

Contents

1 Living Things and Non-living Things

Learning Checklist

- Features of living things
- Features of non-living things
- Natural and man-made things

Let's Get Started

Look at the pictures shown below. Some of them are living things and some are non-living things. List their names under the appropriate column in the table given below.

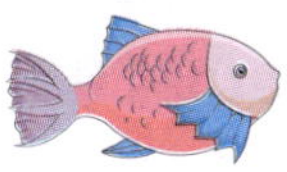
Fish

Books

Mobile phone

Giraffe

Elephant

Living Things	Non-living Things

Lion

Bus

Pencil

Table

We see many things around us. Some of them are living things, while some are non-living things.

Things that breathe, grow, eat food, move on their own, feel, reproduce and excrete waste are called **living things**. All animals, plants and human beings are *living things*.

FEATURES OF LIVING THINGS

There are certain features of living things that make them different from non-living things. Let us study these features.

Living Things Breathe

All living things need air to breathe. We breathe in air through our **nose**. Many animals such as cow, dog and tiger also breathe through their nose. Insects such as cockroach, butterfly and mosquito breathe through **air holes** in their body. Fish live in water and breathe through **gills**.

A dog breathes through its nose

A fish breathes through its gills

Plants breathe through tiny holes or openings called **stomata** (singular: stoma) present on the underside of their leaves.

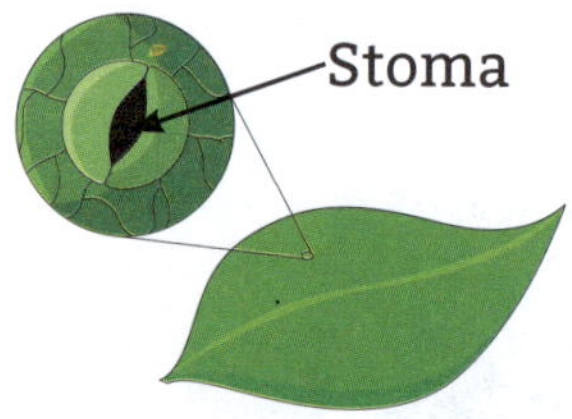

Underside of leaf showing a stoma

Living Things Excrete Waste

Plants give out excess water and gases through leaves. Animals give out impure air and wastes such as undigested food from their body. Sweat is given out by human beings as a waste product.

A plant giving out excess water through leaves

Living Things Move

Living things can move from one place to another in search of food and shelter. Animals walk and run with their **legs**. Birds fly using their **wings**. Fish swim with their **fins**.

A bird flies using its wings

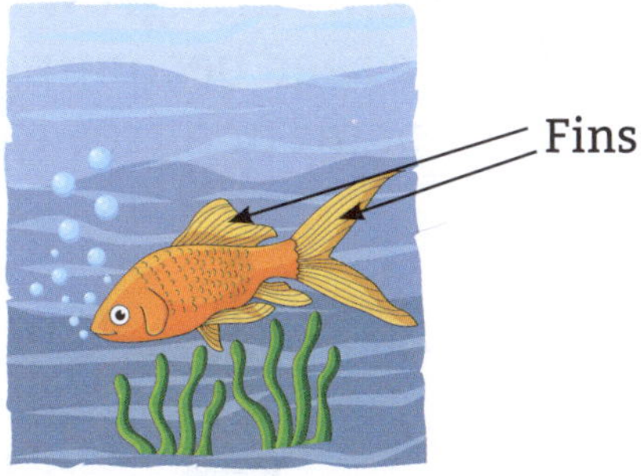

A fish swims with its fins

Plants do not move like animals from place to place, but they show movements with their body parts. For example, the leaves of a *Mimosa* plant curl up when we touch them. Hence, it is called the 'touch-me-not' plant.

Leaves of *Mimosa* plant

Folded leaves of *Mimosa* plant when touched

Living Things Need Food

All living things need food to live and grow. Green plants make their own food using air, water, soil and sunlight. Human beings, animals and birds depend on plants and other animals for their food.

A bird feeding on an insect

A sheep eating grass

Living Things Grow

All living things grow. Look at your childhood pictures. You will see that you are much taller now than when you were a baby. You have grown from being a baby to a child. Plants also grow. Growth of a plant starts from a seed becoming a seedling[1] and then into a plant or a tree to bear fruits.

Word Web

[1]**Seedling:** a young plant that grows from a seed

A baby grows into an adult.

A kitten grows into a cat.

A seedling grows into a plant.

Revise and Recall

Fill in the blanks using the correct words.

1. Dogs use their __________ to breathe. (mouth/nose)
2. Fish swim in water using their __________. (fins/gills)
3. Living things need __________ to live and grow. (food/flowers)
4. A bird eats grains, fruits and __________. (insects/stones)
5. A kitten __________ into a cat. (grows/eats)

Living Things Feel

All living things can feel or respond to changes around them. We have ears to hear sounds, eyes to see things around us, nose to breathe and smell, tongue to taste food and skin to feel touch and pain.

All these body parts make up the **sense organs** in humans and animals.

Wounded boy crying

A girl smelling flowers

Sense organs help us to feel changes around us. Happiness, pain, hunger, sadness, fear, etc. are all different feelings.

Plants can also feel changes around them. For example, plants grow towards the source of light.

Scared boy running

A happy boy

A plant growing towards the sun

Insects such as cockroach and butterfly have body parts called **antennae**, which help them to feel changes around them.

Cockroach

Living Things Reproduce

All living things reproduce. The process in which living things produce young ones of their own kind is called **reproduction**. Most of the plants reproduce by producing seeds that give rise to another plant of the same kind when sown in the soil. Some plants reproduce from their roots, stems or leaves.

Animals reproduce by laying eggs or by giving birth to baby animals or young ones of their own kind. For example, a hen lays eggs from which chicks come out while a cow gives birth to a calf.

Seed of a plant produces another plant

A cow with its calf

A mother with her child

FEATURES OF NON-LIVING THINGS

Some features of non-living things are as follows:

- Non-living things do not breathe or need food.
- Non-living things do not excrete waste.
- They cannot move on their own. For example, a car can move only if someone drives it.
- They do not feel or respond to changes around them.
- They do not grow or reproduce.

NATURAL AND MAN-MADE THINGS

a

Living things and non-living things found in nature are called **natural things**. Sunlight, water, air, rocks and plants are some examples of natural things. Living things need light from the sun, air to breathe and water to drink.

Human beings build non-living things such as aeroplanes, houses, buildings and bridges across rivers. The non-living things built by humans are called **man-made things**.

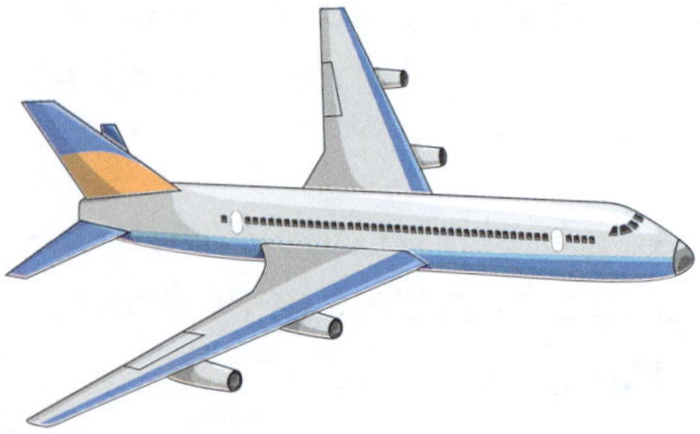

An aeroplane

A house

Keywords

Living things: Things that breathe, move on their own, need food, excrete waste, grow, feel and reproduce

Non-living things: Things that do not breathe, move on their own, need food, excrete waste, grow, feel and reproduce

Gill: The part of a fish's body that helps it to breathe

Stomata: Small openings on the underside of the leaves that help the plant take in and give out air

Sense organs: The parts of the body that help us to feel changes around us

Reproduction: The process in which living things produce young ones of their own kind

Summary

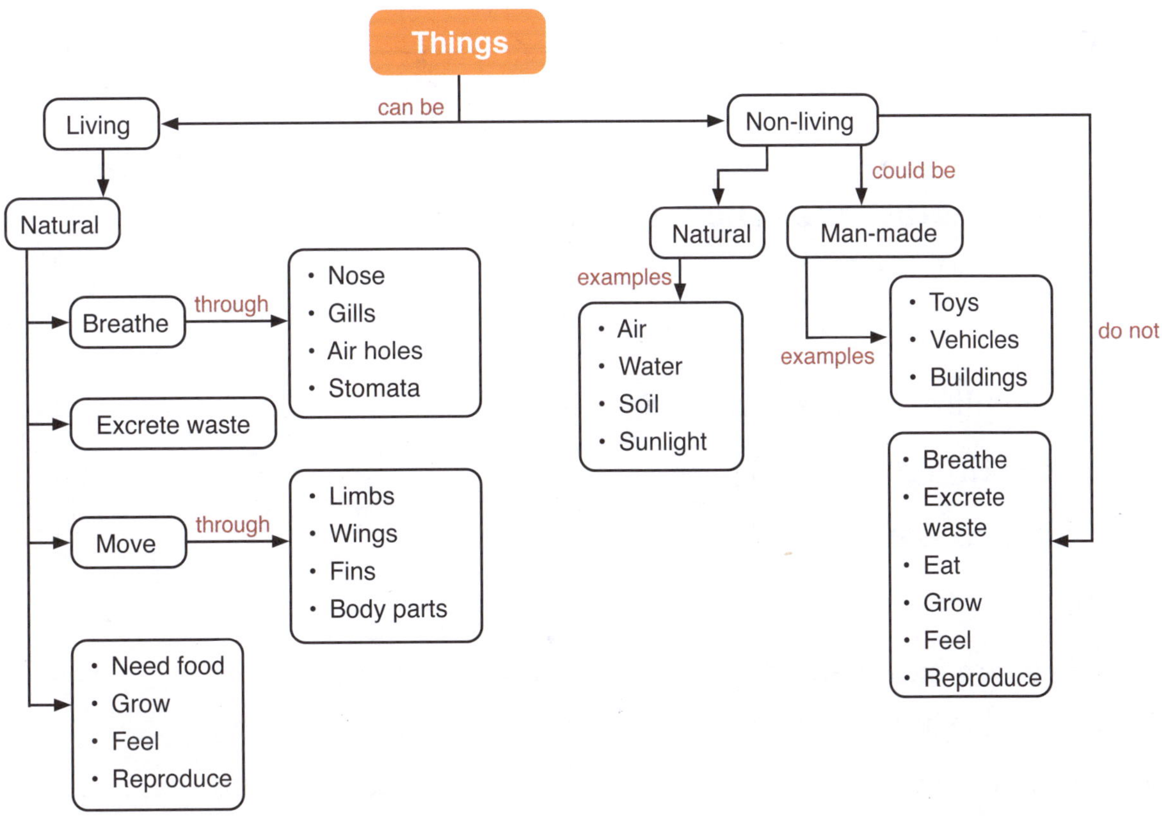

Exercise

W

A. Choose the correct option for each of the following.

1. Insects breathe in air through
   (a) nose (b) gills
   (c) air holes (d) none of these
2. Birds fly with their
   (a) fins (b) wings
   (c) legs (d) gills
3. Which of the following is a natural thing?
   (a) Buildings (b) Bag
   (c) Water (d) Aeroplane

B. Fill in the blanks using the correct words. ia

1. Living things need ________________ to breathe. (air/water)
2. Plants breathe through ________________. (gills/stomata)
3. We can hear sounds with our ________________. (nose/ears)
4. A coconut tree is a ________________ thing. (living/non-living)
5. A cup is a ________________ thing. (natural/man-made)

C. State whether the following statements are true (T) or false (F). ia

1. Birds do not need food to live. ☐
2. Green plants make their own food. ☐
3. Living things can feel pain. ☐
4. Animals do not feel changes around them. ☐
5. Man-made things are living things. ☐

D. Give two examples for each of the following.

1. Animals that use nose to breathe ________ and ________
2. Sense organs ________ and ________

3. Insects that have antennae __________ and __________
4. Animals that give birth to young ones __________ and __________
5. Natural things __________ and __________

E. Give reasons for the following.

1. Babies cry when they fall down.
2. Sweat is given out by human beings.
3. Animals need to move from place to place.
4. A car can move only if someone drives it.
5. Insects such as cockroach and butterfly have body parts called antennae.

F. Answer the following questions briefly.

1. Name the parts of the body used by birds and fish to move.
2. Why do living things need food?
3. How do green plants make their food?
4. How do plants reproduce?
5. What are man-made things?

G. Answer the following questions.

1. How are living things different from non-living things?
2. Give one example of movement in plants.
3. Name the sense organs and their functions.
4. What is reproduction?

Cognitive Corner

Critical Thinking

1. Fiza decided to try on the clothes that her mother purchased when she was young. She was surprised to see that the clothes do not fit her now. Why is she not able to fit into those clothes?
2. You must have seen a fish aquarium which is a home for fish. Is it man-made or natural?

Picture Study

Write which feature of living things is shown in the following pictures.

Elephant and its baby in the picture show that living things can

____

Plants in the pots show that living things can

____

Project

1. Make a list of all the non-living things that you use starting from brushing your teeth in the morning to sleeping at night. Collect the pictures of these things and paste them in a scrapbook.
2. Unscramble the following sense organs.

(a) SOEN (b) KSNI (c) SERA (d) UGNTOE (e) YESE

Life Skills

Sahnaz, Peter, Basu and Parul are planting a sapling each.

(a) Suggest two ways to take care of these saplings.

(b) Can they grow more plants in the same area? Justify your answer.

Worksheet

Oxygen is a gas that is needed by all living things to live. We breathe in oxygen present in the air through our noses. Plants too need oxygen to breathe. Animals and plants living under water take in oxygen that is dissolved in water.

Whales and dolphins are like us. They cannot take in dissolved oxygen. They breathe in air with their lungs, like we do.

Dolphin

Whale

Let us see how they breathe.

A dolphin has nostrils called blowholes on the top of its head. It comes to the surface of the water from time to time to breathe through its blowhole. It breathes out (exhales) first and then breathes in (inhales) fresh air. Dolphins are able to hold their breath for several minutes but typically they breathe about 4–5 times every minute. Large whales breathe through nostrils, called a blowhole, located right on top of their heads.

Fill in the table below with 'Yes' or 'No' in the correct boxes.

	You	**Fish**	**Dolphin**
Breathe through nose			
Breathe through gills			
Breathe in air			
Breathe in dissolved oxygen			

2 Parts of a Plant

Learning Checklist

- Root system
- Shoot system
- Germination

Let's Get Started

Look at the picture of a plant given below. Name any four parts of a plant.

1. ______________________

2. ______________________

3. ______________________

4. ______________________

Plants are a wonderful gift of nature to human beings. We see many plants around us. They are of different sizes and shapes. Like we have different body parts, a plant also has different parts.

Let us learn more about the different parts of a plant.

PARTS OF A PLANT

a

A plant is divided into two major parts: the root system and the shoot system.

Shoot system: The part of a plant that grows above the ground is called the shoot system. The shoot system consists of stem, branches, leaves, flowers and fruits.

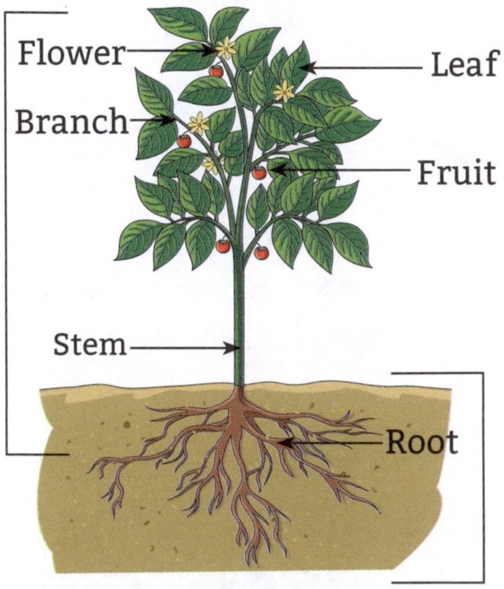

Parts of a plant

Wonder!

There are about 3,50,000 different types of plants on the Earth.

Root system: The part of a plant that grows below the ground is called the root system. The root system consists of roots which fix the plant to the soil.

THE ROOT

It is the underground part of a plant. Roots grow deep into the ground. They also spread wide across the soil in search of water. They hold soil particles and fix the plant firmly into the soil.

There are mainly two types of roots: tap roots and fibrous roots.

Tap root: It has one main root which grows from the base of the stem into the soil. Many small roots grow from the main root. Main root is the first root that appears from the seed. Plants such as bean, carrot and balsam have tap roots.

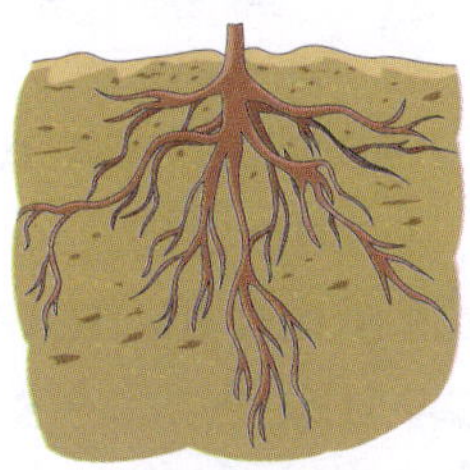
Tap root

Fibrous root

Fibrous root: It is a bunch of small, thin roots that grow from the base of the stem. Some plants that have fibrous roots are grass, paddy and wheat.

Functions of Roots

Word Web

[1]**Absorb:** to take in

- Roots hold the soil particles and help the plants to remain fixed to the soil.
- Roots absorb[1] water, nutrients and minerals from the soil.

- Some roots store food. Plants such as radish, carrot and beetroot store food in their roots. We can eat roots of such plants.

Beetroot

THE STEM

The stem forms the main part of the shoot system. It helps to keep the plant straight and erect. Stems can be of different types. They are soft in young plants. They become hard and strong when plants grow into trees to form the **trunk**. The tender stems are green in colour and the trunks are brown in colour. Some plants such as money plant, watermelon and grapevine have weak stems.

Weak stem

Hard and woody stem

Functions of the Stem

- The stem keeps the plants upright and gives support to them.
- It has many branches that bear leaves, buds, flowers and fruits.
- The stem carries water, food and minerals to all the other parts of a plant.
- Plants such as sugarcane store extra food in the stem. Stems of some plants such as potato and ginger grow under the soil and store the food prepared by them. These underground stems are eaten as food.

Sugarcane

Potato

- Some stems also store water for the plant. Plants such as the desert cacti have thick fleshy stems that store water for the plant.

THE LEAF

It is the most important part of a plant. Most of the leaves are green in colour. They are usually flat, broad and thin. They vary in shapes and sizes.

Parts of a Leaf

Parts of a leaf

1. The flat and broad part of a leaf is called the **leaf blade** or the **lamina**.
2. The line which is seen at the centre of a leaf is called the **main vein** or the **midrib**.
3. The lines present on either side of the main vein are called **side veins**.
4. The part that connects the branch to the leaf is called the **leaf stalk** or the **petiole**.

Science in Context

Leaves purify air by giving out oxygen.

Functions of a Leaf

1. Leaves are called the food factory or the kitchen of a plant because they make food for the plant.
2. Leaves have a green-coloured substance called **chlorophyll** which helps to absorb sunlight.
3. Green leaves prepare food for the plants using air, water and sunlight. This process is called **photosynthesis**.
4. There are tiny openings on the underside of the leaves called **stomata**. They help the plants to breathe.
5. Some plants such as fenugreek (*methi*), mint and spinach store food in their leaves. We eat leaves of such plants.

Fenugreek (*methi*) leaves

Spinach

FLOWERS

Most plants bear flowers. They vary in colour, shape, size and smell. Flowers blossom from buds. They may be single or appear in bunches.

A plant bearing flowers

Functions of Flowers

Most flowers become fruits which contain one or more seeds. The seeds help the plants to reproduce. Cauliflower and broccoli are examples of some flowers that we eat.

FRUITS AND SEEDS

Many plants bear different kinds of fruits. Most fruits have seeds in them. Some fruits have only one seed, while some have many seeds. For example, a watermelon has many seeds, an orange has a few seeds, whereas a mango has only one seed.

Watermelon with many seeds

Mango with one seed

New plants grow from seeds. A seed has a baby plant inside it, which grows into a new plant.

Functions of Fruits and Seeds

- We eat fruits of many plants as they are fleshy, juicy and tasty.
- We eat some seeds such as bean, corn and rice as our food. We also eat some seeds such as pepper and cumin as spices.
- Seeds of rice, wheat and maize are called cereals. Seeds of bengal gram, chickpeas, lentils are called pulses. Cereals and pulses form an important part of our diet.
- A seed stores food for the baby plant.

Revise and Recall

Who am I?

1. I hold the plant firmly into the soil. ____________________
2. I help the plant to stand upright. ____________________
3. I am also called the kitchen of the plant. ____________________
4. I am found inside the fruits. ____________________

GERMINATION

Most plants grow from the seeds. When a seed is buried into the soil, the baby plant inside it starts growing into a new plant when it gets the right amount of water, sunlight and air.

The process of the growth of a new plant from a seed is called **germination**.

Germination of a bean seed

Keywords

Root system: The part of the plant that grows below the ground
Shoot system: The part of the plant that grows above the ground
Tap root: The main root that grows from the base of a stem into the soil
Fibrous root: A bunch of small, thin roots that grow from the base of the stem
Leaf blade: The broad and flat part of a leaf
Petiole: The part that connects the branch to the leaf
Germination: The process of the growth of a seed into a new plant

Summary

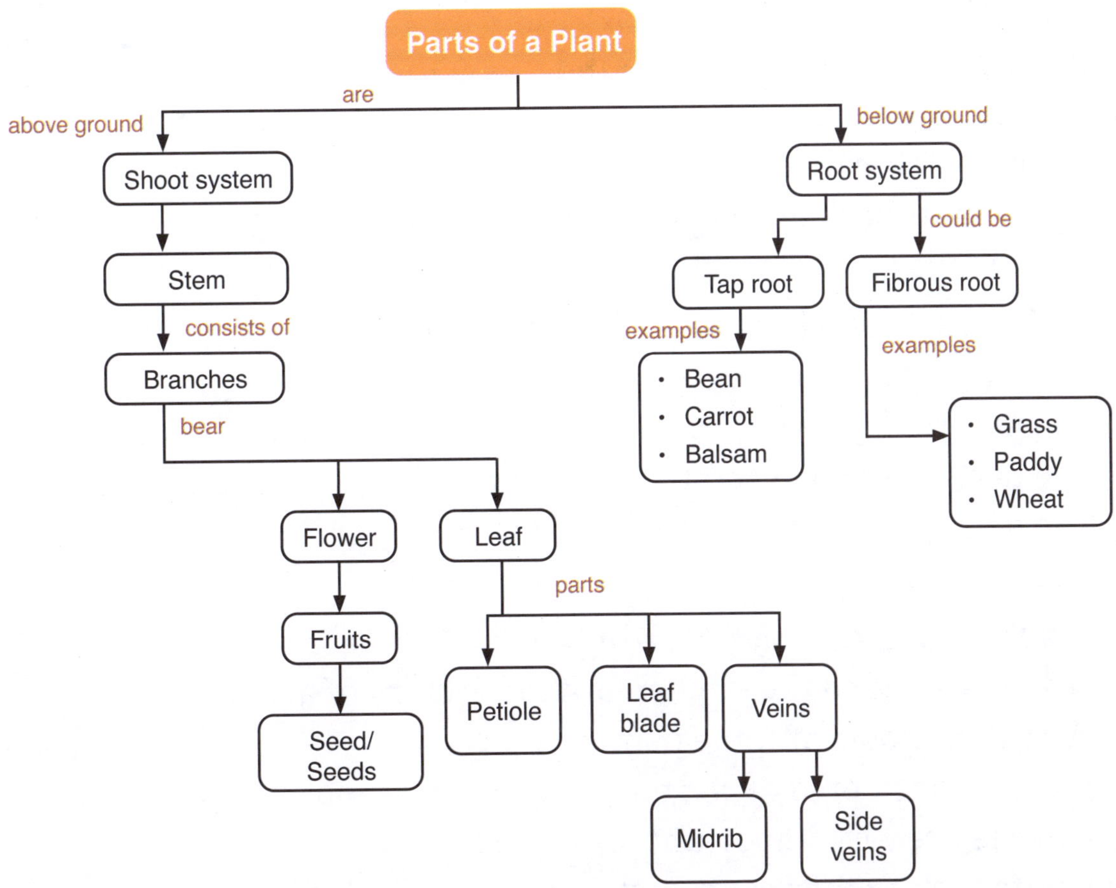

EXERCISE

W

ia

A. Fill in the blanks using the correct words.

1. __________ is the underground part of a plant. (Root/Stem)
2. Carrot and bean have __________ roots. (fibrous/tap)
3. The __________ supports the plant above the ground. (root/stem)
4. Flowers blossom from __________. (buds/roots)
5. A __________ stores food for the baby plant. (seed/stem)

B. Match the following.

	Column A		**Column B**
1.	Wheat	(a)	Edible part of a plant
2.	Balsam	(b)	Trunk
3.	Mint leaves	(c)	Weak stem
4.	Banyan tree	(d)	Fibrous roots
5.	Money plant	(e)	Tap root

C. State whether the following statements are true (T) or false (F).

ia

1. Roots grow deep into the ground. ☐
2. The stem absorbs water and nutrients from the soil. ☐
3. Plants breathe through stomata. ☐
4. Most plants bear flowers which grow into fruits. ☐
5. New plants grow from flowers. ☐

D. Name the following parts of the plant.

1. The part that grows below the ground __________
2. The part that grows above the ground __________
3. The part that makes food for the plant __________
4. The part that becomes a fruit __________
5. The part that contains food for the baby plant __________

E. Give reasons for the following.

1. Leaves are called the kitchen or food factory of a plant.
2. We eat the roots of some plants.
3. Stem is considered as the main part of the shoot system.
4. Flowers are very important for plants.
5. Plants such as the desert cacti have thick fleshy stems.

F. Answer the following questions briefly.

1. What are the two main parts of a plant?
2. What is a tap root? Give one example.
3. What is a midrib?
4. Name two flowers that we eat.
5. What is photosynthesis?

G. Answer the following questions.

1. Write the difference between the root system and the shoot system.
2. Draw a leaf and label its parts.
3. What are the functions of fruits and seeds?

COGNITIVE CORNER

Critical Thinking

Neha ate the seed of a fruit by mistake. Her brother said it will grow into a tree inside her. Do you think this is true? Why/Why not?

Picture Study

Look at the pictures given below and number them in the correct order.

A tiny root begins to grow. | The roots start growing longer into the soil. | A beautiful flower blooms. | A seed is planted. | The first two leaves of the plant grow.

Project

Draw a plant on a chart paper and label its parts. Display the chart in your classroom and speak about the functions of each part.

Life Skills

Collect 5 fallen leaves from a garden. Compare their margins and label the parts of the leaf. Why should we not pluck leaves of a plant?

WORKSHEET

When we cook delicious meals, we use a lot of spices. All spices come from plants. Name any three spices.

________________ ________________ ________________

Garam masala is a blend of ground spices used extensively in Indian cuisine. The spices for *garam masala* are usually toasted to bring out more flavour and aroma, and then ground. The word *masala* simply means spices and *garam* means hot.

Some of the spices used for making *garam masala* are given below. Find out the part of the plant that is the source of these spices.

STEM FLOWER SEED FRUIT

Cinnamon sticks ________________________

Star anise ________________________

Green cardamom ________________________

Nutmeg ________________________

Cloves ________________________

Collect these from your kitchen and smell them. Name two dishes that are prepared using these spices.

________________________ ________________________

3 What Animals Eat

Learning Checklist

- Eating habits of animals
- How do animals eat?
- Food chain

Let's Get Started

Write the name of the favourite food item of each animal shown below.

____

____

____

____

Animals need food to grow and stay healthy. Food provides energy to the animals so that they can move around and do various activities. Let us learn more about the eating habits of animals.

EATING HABITS OF ANIMALS

Different animals eat different kinds of food. The food items that animals eat regularly are called their **eating habits**. Based on the eating habits of animals, they can be broadly divided into five main groups: herbivores, carnivores, omnivores, scavengers and decomposers.

Herbivores

Animals that eat only plants, grass, fruits and vegetables are known as plant-eating animals or **herbivores**. Deer, goat, giraffe, buffalo and horse are examples of herbivores.

Goat

Giraffe

Carnivores

Animals that eat the flesh of other animals are known as flesh-eating animals or **carnivores**. Crocodile, tiger, lion and wolf are examples of carnivores. Animals that are hunted as the food for carnivores are called **prey**. Animals that hunt other animals for food are called **predators**.

Tiger

Wolf

Omnivores

Animals that eat both plants and the flesh of other animals are known as **omnivores**. Bear, crow and dog are examples of omnivores.

Bear

Crow

Science in Context

Human beings are omnivores as they eat plants, plant products, flesh of other animals and animal products.

Scavengers

Animals that eat the flesh of dead animals are called **scavengers**. Hyena and vulture are examples of scavengers.

Vulture

Decomposers

Mushrooms
(a type of fungus)

Organisms that help in decaying or decomposing the remains of dead plants and animals are called **decomposers**. Fungi and bacteria are examples of decomposers.

HOW DO ANIMALS EAT?

We know that different animals have different eating habits. The eating habits of an animal depend mainly on the type of food it eats.

Chewing the Cud

Herbivores such as cow, deer, buffalo and sheep first chew their food once and swallow it. Later, they bring it back to their mouth and chew it for hours. This is referred to as chewing the cud[1].

> **Word Web**
>
> [1]**Cud:** the partially chewed and swallowed food

These animals have strong and broad teeth (biting teeth) in the front to bite off leaves and grass. They also have strong, flat and broad chewing teeth (grinding teeth) at the back, which helps them to chew the food well.

> **Science in Context**
>
> Cows do not have upper front teeth. The upper jaw is covered with a thick layer of hard skin referred to as **dental pad**.
>
> 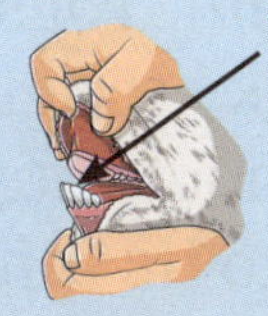
>

Gnawing the Food

Rat

Rabbit

Animals such as squirrel, rabbit and rat have a pair of long, sharp front teeth in the lower and upper jaws. These teeth help them to gnaw[2] seeds, fruits, grains and nuts.

> **Word Web**
>
> [2]**Gnaw:** to keep biting something repeatedly or chew it hard

Tearing the Flesh

Teeth of a carnivore

Carnivores such as tiger, lion and wolf have pointed, sharp, long and curved front teeth (tearing teeth) to tear the flesh. They chew the flesh and bones with their broad and flat grinding teeth at the back of their mouth. They also have strong jaws.

Sucking the Food

A butterfly sucking nectar

Insects such as butterflies and bees have a long, thin tube attached to their mouth. They suck nectar into their mouth from flowers using this tube.

Mosquitoes have sharp, pointed mouth parts with which they suck the blood of animals and humans.

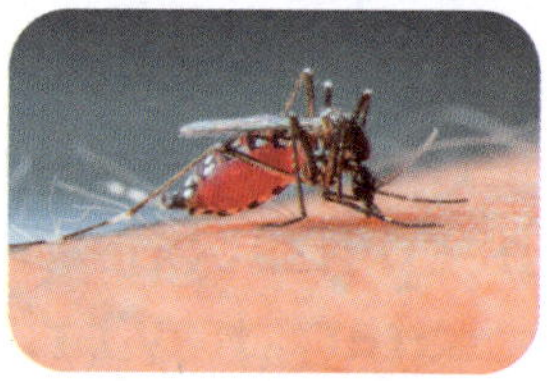
A mosquito sucking blood

Swallowing Food as Whole

Some animals such as snake, lizard and frog do not have any chewing teeth. They swallow their food whole without chewing it.

A frog catching an insect

A snake swallowing its food

Lizards and frogs have a long, sticky tongue. A lizard or frog shoots out its tongue to catch insects. Once the insect gets stuck onto its tongue, it rolls the tongue back into its mouth.

Science in Context

Venomous snakes have sharp curved teeth called fangs. Fangs are used to inject poison (called venom) into the prey.

Fangs

Lapping Up Water or Milk

Animals such as cat and dog use their tongue to lap up water or milk.

A dog lapping up water

Other Eating Habits

Elephants have a huge, long trunk. It helps them to tear off branches and leaves from trees. They use their trunk to drink water. They also use their trunk to have shower and to lift logs of wood.

An elephant using its trunk to eat food

Earthworms swallow the soil to eat the remains of dead plants and animals present in it. Leeches stick to the body of animals and humans to suck their blood. They have a circular mouth with toothed jaws which helps in sticking onto the skin of the prey.

An earthworm swallowing soil

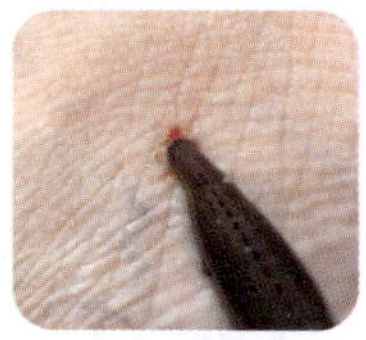

A leech sucking blood

Revise and Recall

State whether the following statements are true (T) or false (F).

1. A rat uses its teeth to gnaw food. ☐
2. Lions have long, sharp and curved teeth to tear the flesh. ☐
3. A cat swallows the whole food without biting and chewing. ☐
4. An elephant uses its trunk only for eating. ☐

FOOD CHAIN

A **food chain** is the chain formed when plants are eaten by animals and then these animals are eaten by other animals. Plants are called the **producers** as they make their own food. A food chain always starts with plants at the lowest level. Hence, all animals—whether herbivores or carnivores—depend directly or indirectly on plants. For example, a grasshopper eats grass, a frog eats the grasshopper and a snake eats the frog.

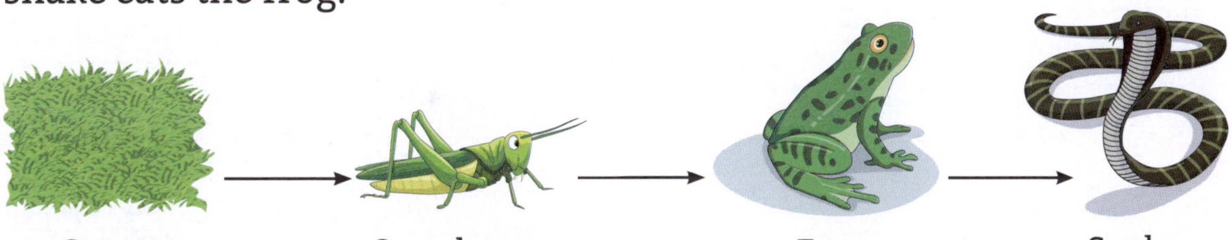

Grass → Grasshopper → Frog → Snake

Keywords

Herbivores: Animals that eat only plants, grass, fruits and vegetables

Carnivores: Animals that eat the flesh of other animals

Omnivores: Animals that eat both plants and the flesh of other animals

Scavengers: Animals that eat the flesh of dead animals

Decomposers: Organisms that decay and decompose the remains of dead plants and animals

Food chain: The chain formed when plants are eaten by animals and then these animals are eaten by other animals

Summary

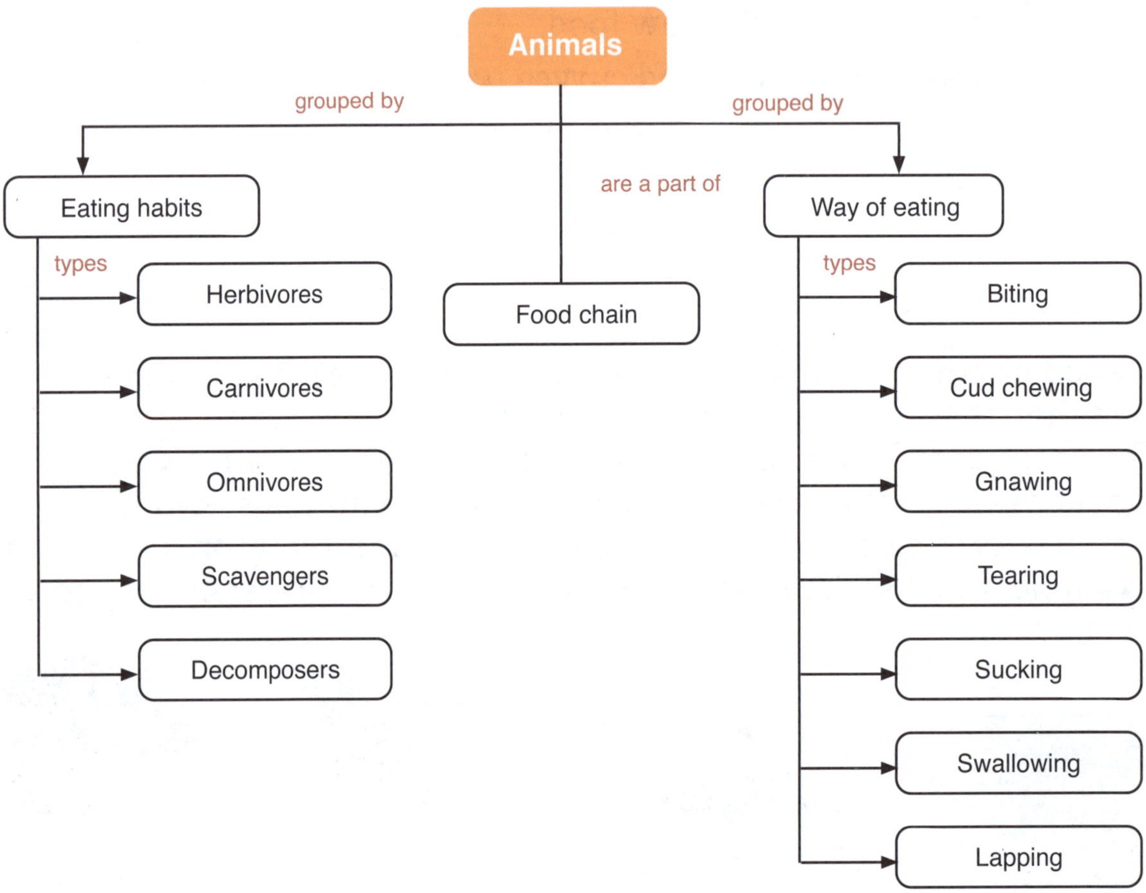

EXERCISE

W

ia

A. Fill in the blanks using the correct words.

1. Plant-eating animals are also called ________. (herbivores/ carnivores)
2. Flesh-eating animals are also called ________. (omnivores/ carnivores)
3. Rabbits ________________ their food. (swallow/gnaw)
4. Frogs ________________ their food. (swallow/tear)
5. Leeches ________________ liquid food. (suck/lap up)

B. Match the following.

	Column A		Column B
1.	Hyena	(a)	Decomposer
2.	Fungi	(b)	Swallowing the whole food
3.	Horse	(c)	Scavenger
4.	Mosquito	(d)	Biting and grinding teeth
5.	Snake	(e)	Sucking tube

C. State whether the following statements are true (T) or false (F).

ia

1. The eating habits of an animal depend upon the type of food it eats. ☐
2. Frog eats both plants and flesh of other animals. ☐
3. Human beings are carnivores. ☐
4. Squirrels gnaw seeds and fruits. ☐
5. Plants are always present at the end of a food chain. ☐

D. Give reasons for the following.

1. Lizards have long and sticky tongue.
2. All living things depend on plants.
3. Squirrels have a pair of long front teeth.
4. Mosquitoes have a sharp and pointed mouth part.
5. Carnivores and herbivores have strong grinding teeth.

E. Answer the following questions briefly.

1. Why do animals need food?
2. What are omnivores? Give two examples.

3. What are scavengers?
4. What are decomposers? Give an example.
5. How do butterflies and mosquitoes eat their food?
6. How is the trunk useful for the elephants?

F. Answer the following questions.

1. Differentiate between herbivores, carnivores and omnivores.
2. Distinguish between chewing the cud and tearing the food.
3. What kind of eating habits do leeches and earthworms have?
4. Define food chain with the help of an example.

COGNITIVE CORNER

Critical Thinking

Tiger and snake are flesh-eating animals but both have different eating habits. Give reason for your answer.

Picture Study

Identify the odd animal from the pictures given below.

Project

Collect pictures of different animals and paste them in your scrapbook. Write about their eating habits and group them as herbivores, carnivores, omnivores, scavengers or decomposers.

Life Skills

Put a tick mark (✓) against the correct statements and cross (✗) against the wrong ones.

(a) We should not harm the animals. ☐

(b) We should tease the animals. ☐

(c) We should provide enough water for the animals to drink. ☐

WORKSHEET

Our world has a large variety of animals, a few of which have very strange eating habits.

Ostrich

Ostriches are omnivores. The strange fact is that they eat stones to help them break the food into tiny pieces in the stomach and digest the food.

Chameleons can extend their tongues upto a distance of one and a half times their body length to catch prey.

Chameleon

Crocodile

If its prey is small, a crocodile will swallow it whole without chewing.

A snow monkey washes its food in salt water before eating it.

Snow monkey

Find about the eating habits of the following animals.

Anteater

____

Honeybee

____

4 Birds

Learning Checklist

- Feathers
- How do birds fly?
- Different types of beaks
- Feet and claws
- Where do birds live?

Let's Get Started

a

Look at the picture given below and fill in the missing letters to complete the names of the body parts of the bird. Also, colour the picture.

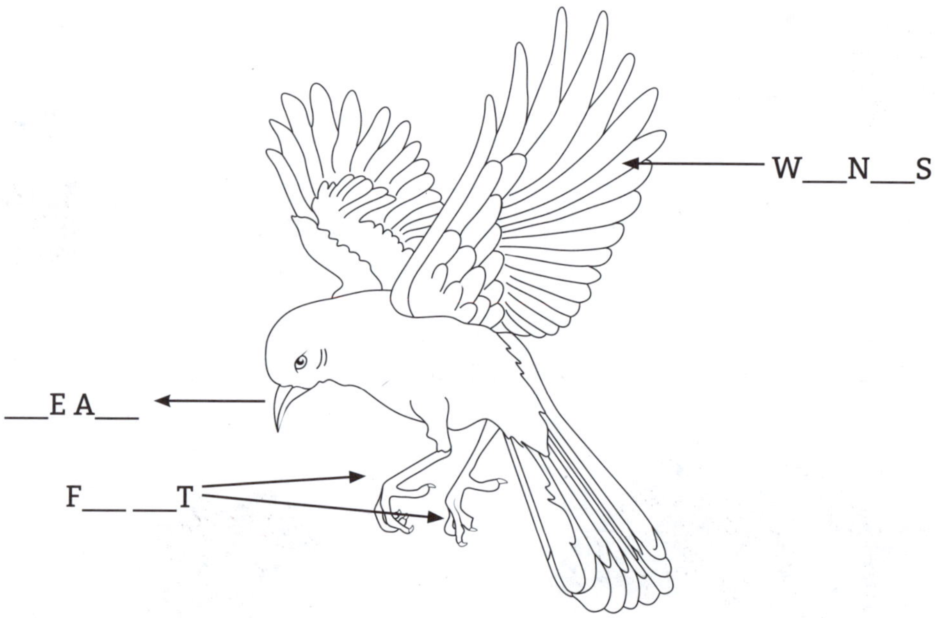

Birds are the animals with their bodies covered with feathers. They have a pair of wings and feet. Birds do not have teeth but they have beaks. Let us learn more about birds.

FEATHERS

Feathers cover the body and wings of birds. Each feather has a central hollow (air filled) shaft with thin hairs on either side.

Birds have three types of feathers. They are:

(a) **Body feathers:** These cover the body of birds and give it a shape.

(b) **Down feathers:** These are short and fluffy feathers which keep the bird's body warm.

(c) **Flight feathers:** These are large feathers found mostly on the wings and tail of a bird. They help the birds to fly. Some birds such as ostrich and emu cannot fly and, hence, are called flightless birds.

Science in Context

Flying birds have light skeleton with many hollow bones which help them to fly. Flightless birds have heavy, solid bones so they cannot lift themselves to fly.

HOW DO BIRDS FLY?

Birds fly with the help of their wings and strong muscles that attach the wings to their body. These muscles are called 'flight muscles'. These help the bird to move its wings up and down or forward and backwards.

Birds have hollow bones which makes their body light. The tail of birds helps in changing their direction while flying. Boat-shaped and light body of the birds help them to cut through the air while flying.

A bird flaps its wings to fly. While flying, the wings show two types of movements:

(a) **Upstroke:** During this movement, the wings move up and backward.

(b) **Downstroke:** During this movement, the wings move down and forward.

A bird flying with upstroke and downstroke movements

DIFFERENT TYPES OF BEAKS

Different birds have different types of beaks. Birds use their beaks to catch and eat food. The shape of the beak is suited to the kind of food they eat.

Strong, Sharp and Hooked Beak

Flesh-eating birds such as eagle, vulture, owl and hawk eat small birds and animals. They have strong, sharp and hooked beaks to tear the flesh of their prey.

Hawk

Vulture

Strong, Sharp and Chisel[1]-shaped Beak

Birds such as woodpecker have strong, sharp and chisel-shaped beaks. Their beaks help them to make holes into the hard tree trunks and pick up insects from these holes.

Woodpecker

Word Web

[1]**Chisel:** a tool with a flat, sharp edge at the end

Strong, Short and Hard Beak

Birds such as sparrow, pigeon, peacock and finch eat seeds, grains and nuts. They have strong, short and hard beaks that help them to crack or crush their food.

Peacock

Sparrow

Long and Slender[2] Beak

Birds such as hoopoe have long and slender beaks that help them to pick up insects from holes in the ground.

Hoopoe

Word Web

[2]**Slender:** thin and narrow

Long, Pointed and Straw-like Beak

Birds such as hummingbird and sunbird have long, pointed and straw-like beaks. Such beaks help them to suck nectar from flowers.

Hummingbird

Sunbird

Science in Context

- Hummingbird is the smallest living bird in the world and it can fly backwards!
- Pelican has a skinny bag under its beak to store fish.

Broad and Flat Beak with Strainers

Birds such as duck and goose have broad and flat beaks with strainers that look like rows of tiny teeth.

These birds take in muddy water containing worms, insects and small water plants. The muddy water goes out through these strainers, leaving the worms, insects and water plants inside their mouth.

Duck

Goose

Short and Broad Beak

Birds such as swallow have short and broad beaks. Swallow flies in the air with its beak open. The inside of its beak is sticky, which helps in catching the flying insects.

Swallow

Hooked and Curved Beak

Birds such as parrot have hooked and curved beaks. Their beaks help them to break open hard fruits and nuts. Parrots can only move their upper beak unlike other birds.

Parrot

Revise and Recall

Choose the correct answer.

1. Which one of the following birds has short and broad beak?
   (a) Swallow (b) Sunbird (c) Sparrow (d) Pigeon
2. Which one of the following birds has long and pointed beak?
   (a) Owl (b) Hummingbird (c) Parrot (d) Peacock
3. Which one of the following birds has hooked and curved beak?
   (a) Hoopoe (b) Parrot (c) Woodpecker (d) Hawk

FEET AND CLAWS

a

Birds have two feet. Each foot has three or four toes. Birds use their claws and feet to hold food. They also use their feet to move around on the ground or on the branches of trees.

Preying Birds

Flesh-eating birds such as eagle, owl and vulture are also called **preying birds**. They have very sharp and curved claws called **talons**. Preying birds have three toes in the front and one at the back. They use their toes to catch small animals such as rats, toads and small birds.

Toes of a vulture

Perching Birds

Birds such as pigeon, crow, sparrow and nightingales have feet with three toes in the front and one behind. Such feet help them to hold on to a branch firmly. This is called **perching**.

Toes of a crow

Scratching Birds

Hens have thin feet with sharp and hard claws. Their claws have three long toes in the front and a short toe at the back, which is higher up the leg. These toes help them to dig the ground and find food. Peacocks also use their toes to dig out food from the ground.

Toes of a hen

Climbing Birds

Birds such as woodpecker and parrot have two toes in the front and two toes at the back. Their toes help them to climb trees and hold onto branches. These also help the birds to balance themselves while climbing.

Toes of a woodpecker

Swimming/Aquatic Birds

Birds such as duck and swan have webbed feet. They have three toes in the front that are joined by skin called **web**. Such webbed feet help them to push back water while swimming.

Toes of a swan

Wading Birds

Birds such as heron and crane have long legs with spread-out toes. These help them to walk in shallow water. This is called **wading**. They have four toes—three in the front and one at the back. Their toes are thin and never get caught in the soft mud.

Long legs of a crane

Running Birds

Ostrich is a runner. It has long and strong legs. It has only two toes with cushion pads underneath, which prevent its legs from sinking in the desert sands.

Toes of an ostrich

Revise and Recall

State whether the following statements are true (T) or false (F).

1. The claws of perching birds are called talons. ☐
2. A woodpecker has two toes in the front and two toes at the back. ☐
3. Wading birds have webbed feet. ☐
4. Emu is a runner. ☐

WHERE DO BIRDS LIVE?

Tailor bird making its nest

The place where birds live with their young ones is called a **nest**. Birds use grass, straw, dry leaves, twigs, pieces of cloth, paper and threads to build their nests.

Birds use their nests to lay and hatch eggs. Nests also help the birds to protect their eggs and young ones from bad weather and enemies.

Birds may build their nests at various places such as on bushes and trees, on roofs of houses and even on the ground.

Weaver bird and its nest

The **tailor bird** uses its beak as a needle to sew leaves together using wool and thread. Hence, it is known as tailor bird. It chooses broad leaves and stuffs them with soft material to make the nest cosy.

The **weaver bird** uses its beak to weave a strong, cup-shaped nest using twigs and dry grass.

The nest usually hangs from the branch of a tree. The nest has a small tunnel-like opening at the bottom from where the bird enters.

The **woodpecker** makes holes in tree trunks with its beak to make a nest.

Penguins make their nests on the ground. Since they live in cold places, it is difficult to find twigs and grass in such places. Hence, they make their nests with pebbles and stones.

Birds such as **fowl** and **partridge** build shallow nest on the ground. They scoop out mud, and spread out straw and hay to make the nest soft and lay eggs. They build nests in grassy fields to remain hidden from predators.

Owl

Penguin with its nest

Owls, **parrots** and **hornbills** build their nests mostly in the hollow spaces of walls or trees.

Cuckoo does not make a nest. It lays its eggs in the crow's nest. The crow looks after its eggs and babies.

> **Science in Context**
>
> The study of birds is called ornithology.

Terns make nests by spinning around on the sand. **Flamingos** make mud piles and lay eggs on the top of the pile. **Swifts** use their saliva to glue sand and form beautiful nests on walls.

Kingfisher makes a tunnel-shaped nest. It digs a long tunnel on the bank of a river or pond. It makes its nest cosy by spreading fish bones on it.

Caring for the Young Ones

The mother bird lays its eggs in its nest and keeps them warm until they hatch into young ones. The father bird helps to protect the eggs from enemies. Once the babies hatch out, they cannot fly as they are weak, featherless and cannot see. So, the parent birds help them by feeding. They take care of their young ones until they develop feathers, and learn to fly and search for food on their own.

Mother bird feeding its young ones

Keywords

Talons: The sharp and curved claws of flesh-eating birds

Flight muscles: Muscles that attach the wings to the bird's body and help in flying

Upstroke: The movement of wings in upward and backward directions

Downstroke: The movement of wings in downward and forward directions

Nest: The place where the birds live with their young ones

Summary

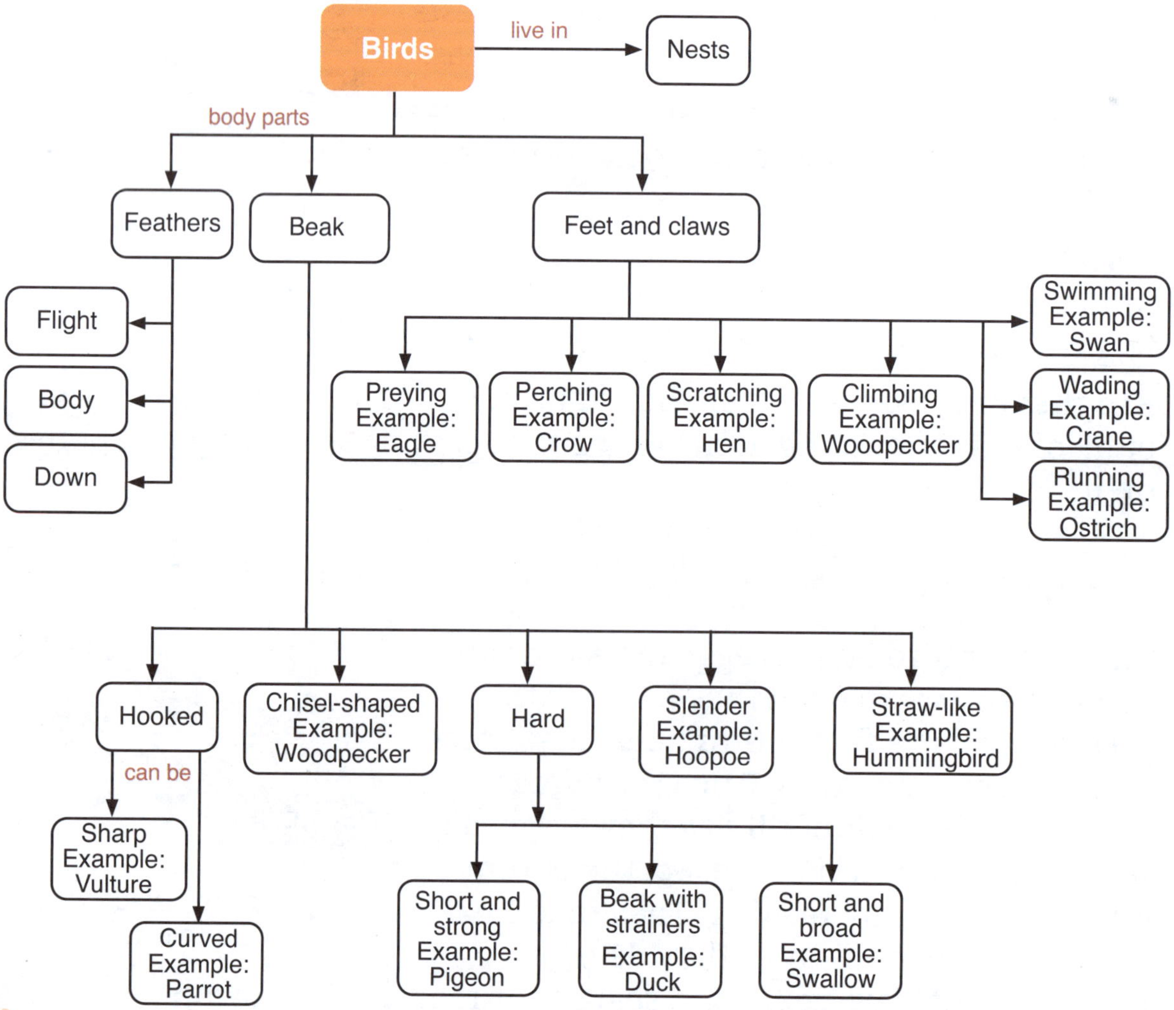

EXERCISE

W

A. Fill in the blanks using the correct words. ia

1. Birds have ________ feet. (four/two)
2. Heron and crane are examples of ________ birds. (wading/scratching)
3. ________ feathers help the birds to fly. (Flight/Down)
4. Flesh-eating birds are also called ________ birds. (preying/wading)
5. ________ does not make a nest. (Cuckoo/Crow)

B. State the following statements as true (T) or false (F). ia

1. The type of beak a bird has depends on its feeding habit. ☐
2. Hummingbird has long, pointed and straw-like beak. ☐
3. Flight feathers are present mostly on the wings and tail of a bird. ☐
4. All birds make nests and live in it. ☐
5. As soon as the babies hatch out of the eggs, they fly away. ☐

C. Give two examples for each of the following.

1. Birds with sharp and hooked beak ________ and ________
2. Birds with broad and flat beak with strainers ________ and ________
3. Preying birds ________ and ________
4. Climbing birds ________ and ________
5. Birds that build shallow nests on the ground ________ and ________

D. Give reasons for the following.

1. Emu is a flightless bird.
2. Body and down feathers of a bird are as important as flight feathers.
3. The toes of ostrich have cushion pads.
4. Crow is called a perching bird.
5. The beaks of ducks are broad and flat with strainers.

E. Answer the following questions briefly.

1. What are talons?
2. What is the use of webbed feet in birds?
3. What is the difference between flight feathers and down feathers?

4. Why do birds build nests?
5. What are the various materials used by birds to build their nests?

F. Answer the following questions.

1. Why do birds have different types of beaks? Give any three examples.
2. How do scratching birds differ from perching birds?
3. How do birds fly? Explain in detail.
4. Explain how a tailor bird's nest is different from a weaver bird's nest.
5. Explain how birds take care of their young ones.

COGNITIVE CORNER

Critical Thinking

Vultures have curved claws called talons, whereas ducks have webbed feet. Why? Give reason for your answer.

Picture Study

Circle the odd one from the pictures given below.

Project

Collect pictures of various birds. Group all the pictures based on the type of beaks, and the type of claws and feet they have. Paste them in your scrapbook. Write about the type of nests they live in. Display your scrapbook in your classroom.

Life Skills

Put a tick mark (✓) against the correct statements and cross (✗) against the wrong statements.

(a) We should not harm the birds. ☐

(b) We can destroy any of the bird's nests. ☐

(c) We should not tease any bird during birdwatching. ☐

WORKSHEET

For many centuries, humans have tried to fly just like the birds. Wings made of feathers or light weight wood have been attached to arms to test their ability to fly. The results were often disastrous as the muscles of human arms are not like that of the bird's.

On December 17, 1903, Wilbur and Orville Wright invented the first successful airplane. Humankind was now able to fly! During the next century, many new airplanes and engines were developed to help transport people, luggage, cargo, military personnel and weapons.

An aeroplane

Birds have a streamlined body shape. Due to this streamlined shape, the air flows on their surface smoothly when they are in flight. Engineers and scientists used the shape of the birds as inspiration to model the planes.

Compare birds and aeroplanes.

Streamlined body of a fighter jet

Streamlined body of a bird

A. In what ways is a plane similar to a bird?

____

____

____

B. How is a bird different from a plane?

____

____

____

5 Our Body

Learning Checklist

- What is the body made up of?
- Organ systems
- Exercise and rest
- Posture

Let's Get Started

Look at the pictures given below and write the names of the body parts that are being used to perform the activities mentioned.

Eyes Nose Tongue Feet Hands

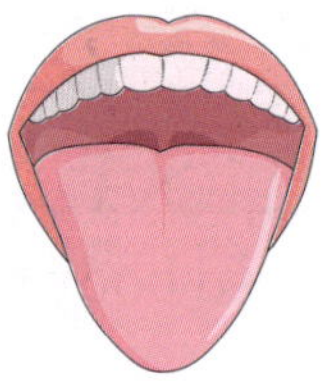

I taste with my ________ .

I write with my ________ .

I smell the beautiful flowers with my ________ .

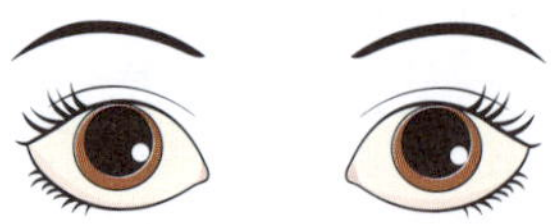

I see the world around me with my ________ .

I kick the ball with my ________ .

WHAT IS THE BODY MADE UP OF?

Our body is made up of very small parts called **cells**. Our body grows from a single cell. Cells multiply and give rise to many cells, which build up the body. Hence, cells are the building blocks of a living body.

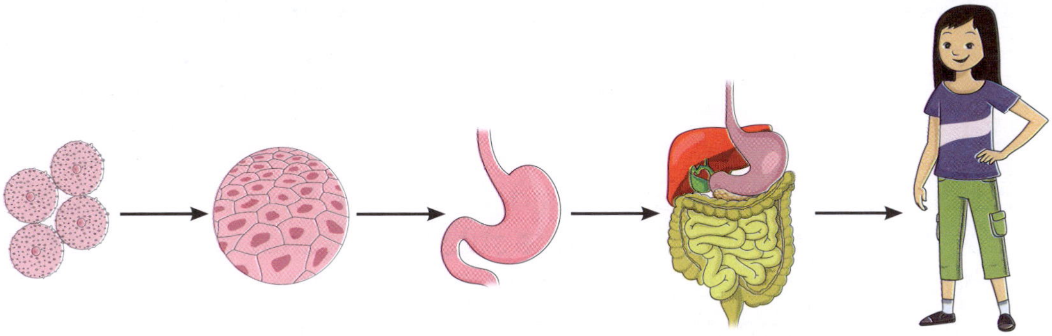

A **cell** is the smallest part of a living body.	A **tissue** is made up of many cells.	An **organ** is made up of different tissues.	Many organs are grouped together to form an **organ system**.	Different organ systems make up an **organism**.

ORGAN SYSTEMS

The human body is made up of many organs. A group of organs work together to form an organ system. Every organ system in the body carries out a particular function to keep the body fit and healthy.

Skeletal System

The bones in our body form the skeletal system. There are 206 bones in an adult human body. The bones together form a structure called the **skeleton**.
The skeletal system gives shape and support to our body. It also protects the internal organs and helps in the movement of our body.

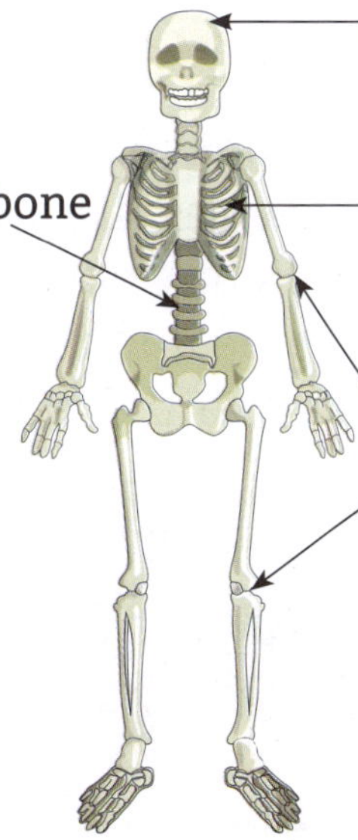

Skeletal system

Science in Context

A newborn baby has more than 206 bones in its body. Some bones join as the baby grows into an adult.

Muscular System

The muscles in our body form the muscular system. Muscles work along with the bones to give shape to the body and help the body parts move. There are more than 600 muscles in the human body.

> **Science in Context**
>
> Organs such as heart and stomach are made up of only muscles.

Digestive System

The food that we eat is digested inside our body. **Digestion** is the process of breaking food into simple substances that can be used by our body. The organs that help in digestion form the digestive system. The food in mouth enters the stomach through the food pipe. The stomach holds the food and breaks it down so that our body can use it to get energy. The small intestine digests the food further. The remaining undigested part is removed from our body through the large intestine and anus.

Respiratory System

The nose, the windpipe and the lungs make up the respiratory system. The respiratory system helps us to breathe. We breathe in air through our nose or mouth. The air then goes down through the windpipe and reaches the lungs. The air we breathe in is called **inhaled air** and the air we breathe out is called **exhaled air**.

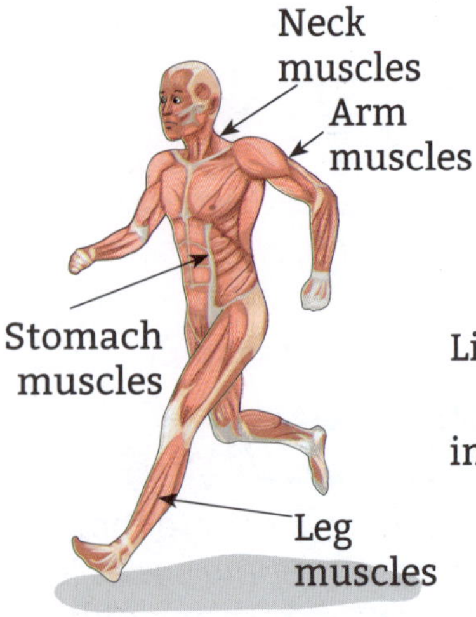

Muscular system

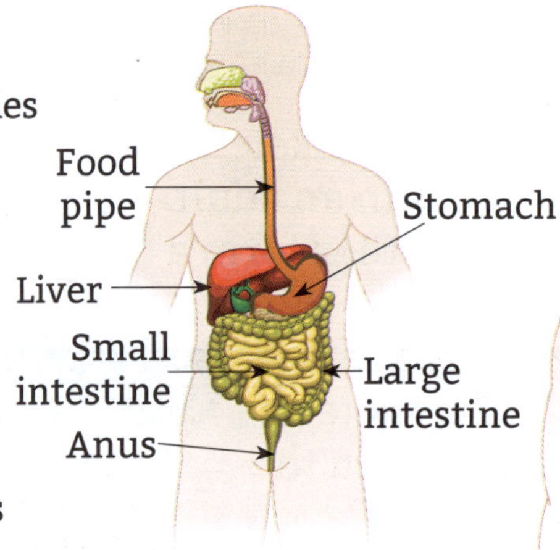

Digestive system

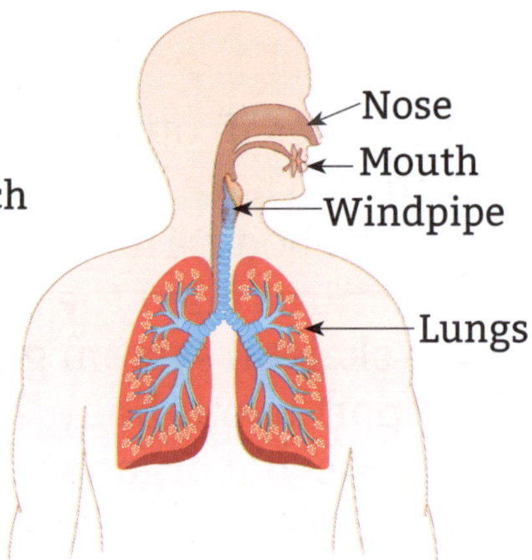

Respiratory system

Nervous System

The brain, the spinal cord and the nerves form the nervous system. The brain controls the whole body and tells it what to do. The spinal cord starts from the brain and connects all the nerves in the body to the brain. These nerves receive information from the brain and pass it to the bones, muscles and other body parts. They also carry messages back to the brain.

Circulatory System

The heart, the blood and the blood vessels form the circulatory system. The heart pumps blood to all parts of the body, which is carried by thin tubes called **blood vessels**. The blood carries nutrients and gases such as oxygen and carbon dioxide to different parts of the body.

Excretory System

The organs that remove wastes such as urine, sweat, etc. produced in the body form the excretory system. The kidneys remove wastes from the blood and form urine. The urine is stored in the urinary bladder and comes out through the urethra. The skin removes sweat and the lungs give out carbon dioxide and some amount of water vapour.

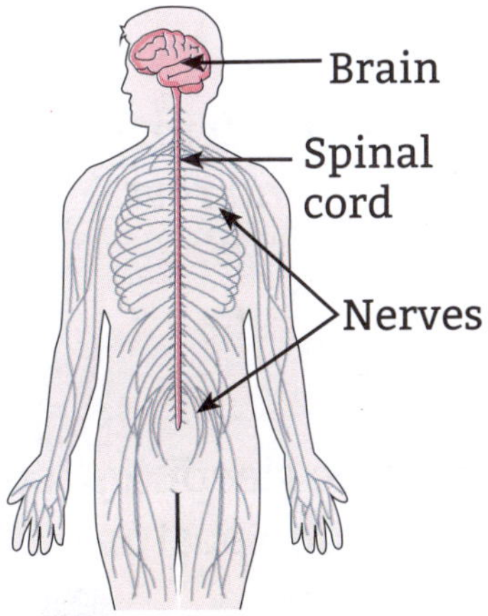

Nervous system

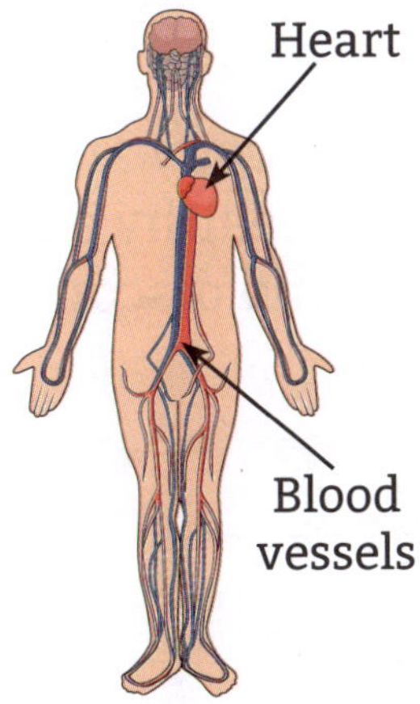

Circulatory system

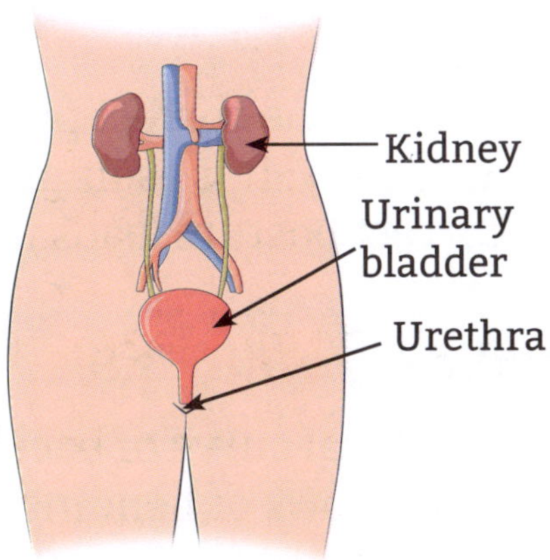

Excretory system

Reproductive System

The reproductive system helps to produce babies or young ones.

Revise and Recall

What am I made up of?

1. The skeletal system ______________________________
2. The muscular system ______________________________
3. The digestive system ______________________________
4. The nervous system ______________________________

EXERCISE AND REST

We should exercise regularly as it keeps our body fit and healthy. Yoga, jogging and playing are different forms of exercise.

We feel tired after a day's hard work or after playing games. It is important to take rest and relax our body. We also need enough sleep at night to feel fresh the next morning.

Exercise regulary

Our body becomes unfit if we do not exercise regularly or take enough rest and sleep.

POSTURE

Posture is the correct position of a body and its parts while performing any activity. It is as important as healthy eating, exercise and rest. Incorrect posture leads to aches and discomfort.

Posture While Sleeping

The natural curve of backbone has to be maintained while sleeping. Too many pillows or bending or curling the body might spoil the posture.

Posture While Walking

We should walk with straight body, eyes looking forward, chin up and, relaxed and open shoulder. Slouched posture can cause physical pain and discomfort.

Keywords

Cell: The building blocks of a living body

Digestion: The process of breaking food into simple substances that can be used by our body

Blood vessels: Thin tubes inside the body through which blood flows to different body parts

Posture: The position of the body while sitting, standing or walking

Summary

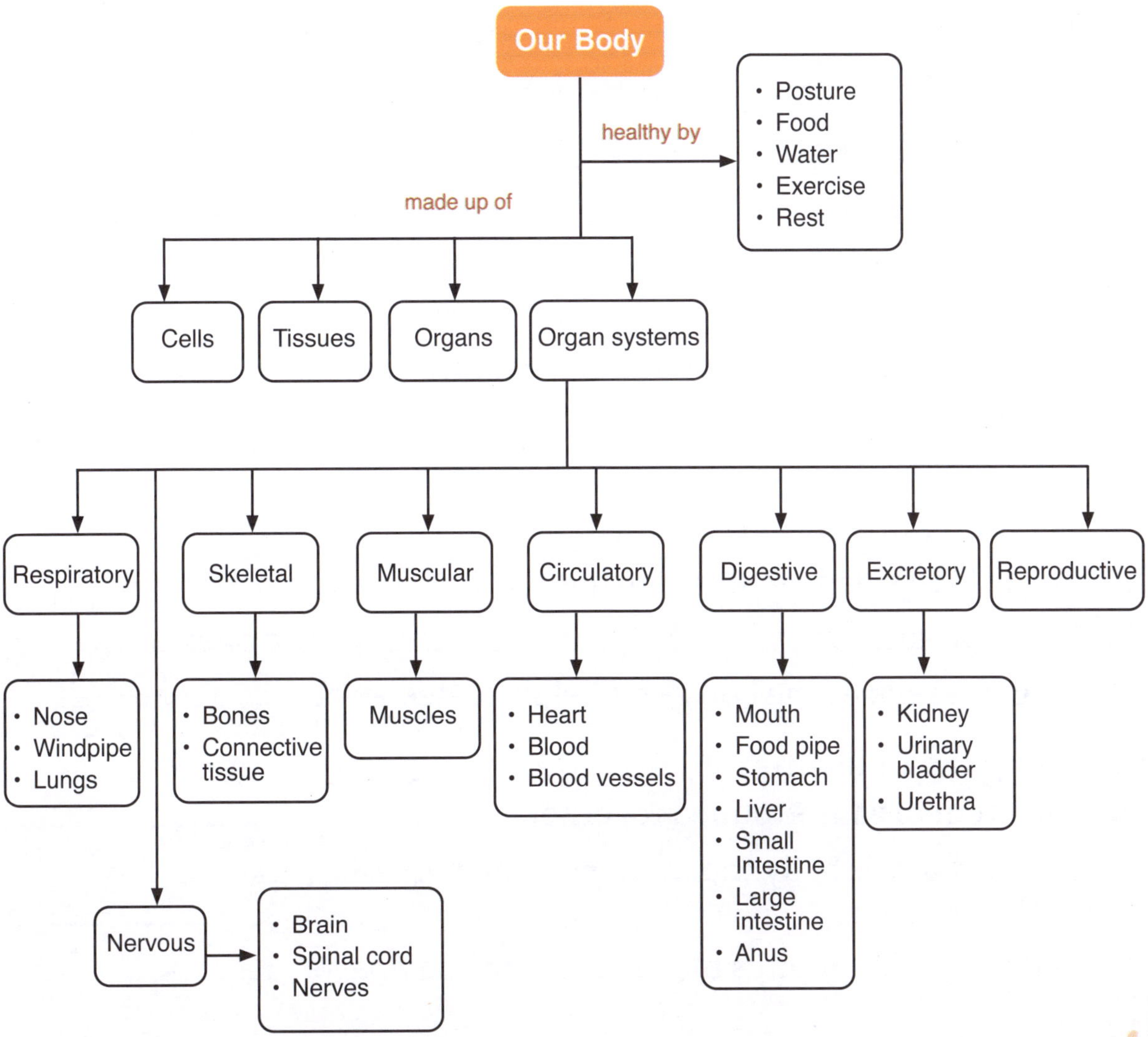

EXERCISE

W

ia

A. Fill in the blanks using the correct words.

1. The smallest part of our body is called a ______________ . (cell/tissue)
2. All the bones together form the ______________. (skeleton/muscles)
3. The air we breathe in goes down through the ______________ . (windpipe/lungs)
4. The ______________ pumps blood to all parts of the body. (lungs/heart)
5. Exercise makes the body ______________ . (healthy/fat)

B. Match the following.

	Column A		Column B
1.	Excretory system	(a)	Lungs
2.	Respiratory system	(b)	Stomach
3.	Circulatory system	(c)	Brain
4.	Digestive system	(d)	Kidneys
5.	Nervous system	(e)	Heart

C. State whether the following statements are true (T) or false (F).

ia

1. Different organ systems make up an organ. ☐
2. The air we breathe out is called inhaled air. ☐
3. The urinary bladder stores urine. ☐
4. The reproductive system helps in producing young ones. ☐
5. Exercise relaxes the body and helps us sleep well. ☐

D. Name the following.

1. Different organs grouped together ______________
2. The part of the body that connects the nerves to the brain ______________
3. The organ that pumps blood to all the body parts ______________

4. The thin tubes through which blood flows ____________

5. The part of the body that forms urine ____________

E. Give reasons for the following.

1. Cells are the building blocks of a living body.
2. Lungs are a part of respiratory as well as excretory system.
3. Skeleton system is important for our body.
4. We need enough sleep at night.

F. Answer the following questions briefly.

1. What is a cell?
2. What is the function of the skeletal system?
3. How do muscles help us?
4. Which organs make up the respiratory system?
5. Why is exercising important?

G. Answer the following questions.

1. Define digestion. Name and write the functions of the organs that make up the digestive system.
2. Write a note on the nervous system.
3. Explain the circulatory system.
4. Why and when is it important to have a good posture?

COGNITIVE CORNER

Critical Thinking

1. Does your brain sleep or rest when you sleep?
2. Kavita thinks that the cooking gas in her house is leaking. Which sense organ helped her notice the leak?

Picture Study

Match the body parts with their names. One has been done for you.

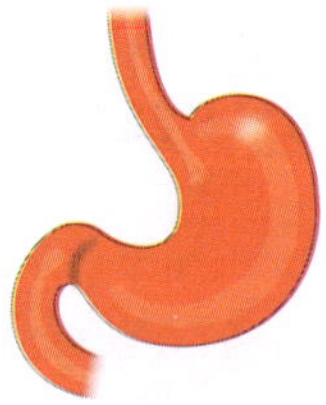

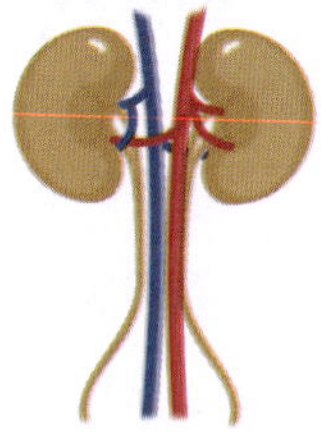

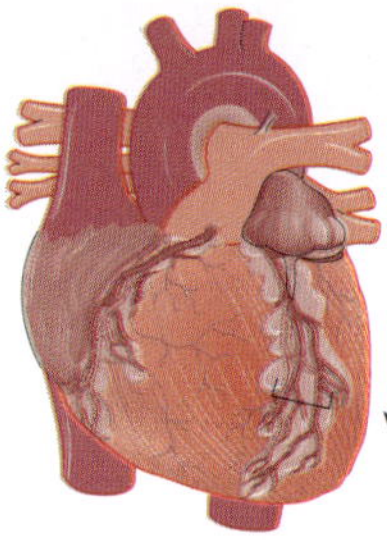

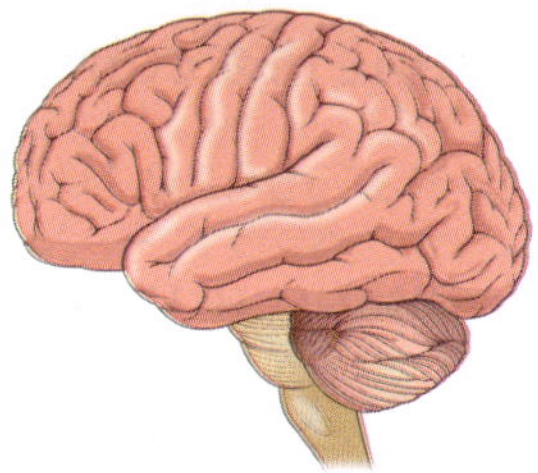

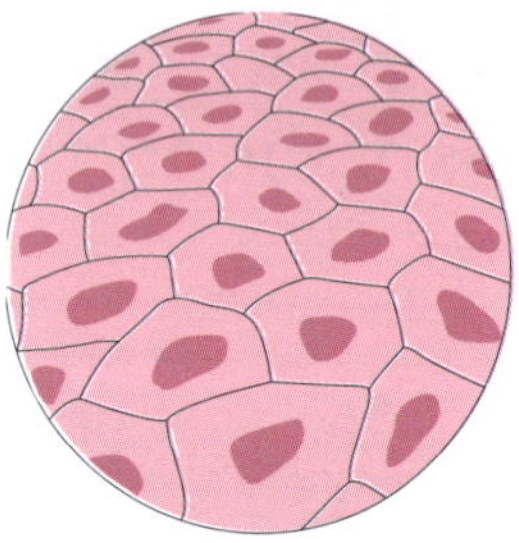

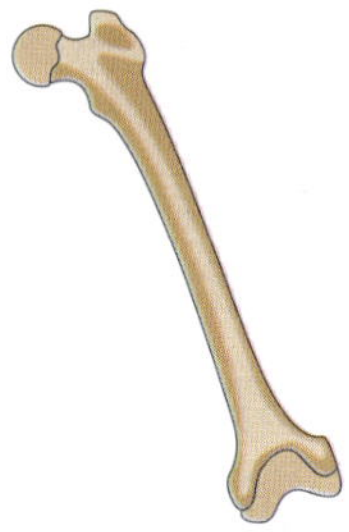

Tissues

Kidneys

Stomach

Brain

Bone

Heart

Project

Draw a labelled diagram of the digestive system on a chart paper and display it in your class.

Life Skills

Drinking enough water is essential along with exercise, rest and right posture.

(a) How many glasses of water do you drink per day?

(b) How many hours do you sleep every day?

(c) Do you exercise and maintain a good posture all the time? If yes, what kind of exercise or sports activity do you like to do?

WORKSHEET

Animals sense the environment with sensory organs, such as eyes, ears, and noses. Sensory organs are vital for animals to find food and avoid danger. Humans have five basic senses—sight, hearing, smell, taste and touch. Animals use the same senses, though sometimes in different ways. Some animals even have extra senses that humans don't possess.

Here are some examples of how some animals sense the outside world.

Bat

Bats have a special feature called nose-leaf, which helps them to detect an animal from about 16 cm away.

The eyes of the chameleon can move independently. Therefore, it can see in two different directions at the same time.

Chameleon

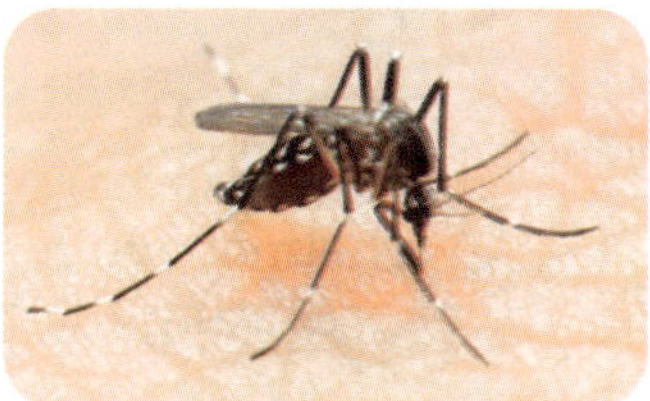

Mosquito

Mosquitoes are attracted by smell of the human body (especially the smell of the foot) and body heat.

Snakes have no external ears. They hear by detecting movements on the ground.

Snake

Do you know that the tongue of a snake has no taste buds? How do snakes taste their food? Find out.

____

____

6 Keeping Safe

Learning Checklist

- Safety at home and in school
- Safety on the road and in the playground
- First aid

Let's Get Started

Read the conversation given below and tick (✓) the safe situations and cross out (✗) the unsafe situations.

Keeping safe means staying away from harm or injury. We may get hurt or injured if we are not careful at all times. We must follow some safety rules to avoid injuries and accidents.

Let us learn some ways to keep ourselves safe.

SAFETY AT HOME

a

We should follow some safety rules to avoid injuries at home.

- Do not take any medicine on your own without asking an elder or a doctor.
- Do not touch electric switches, plugs or wires with wet hands. You might get an electric shock.
- Do not fly kites on an open terrace or burst crackers near electric poles and wires.
- Be careful while walking on wet bathroom floor. You or someone else might slip and get hurt.
- Do not leave toys, bags, shoes or other things scattered on the floor/on the staircase. You or someone else might trip over them and get hurt.
- Do not play with lit candles or matchsticks.
- Do not go near the stove. You might get a burn.
- Do not play with sharp objects such as scissors and knife. You might injure yourself.
- Do not wear synthetic clothes while lighting firecrackers as they tend to catch fire easily.

SAFETY IN SCHOOL

We should follow some safety rules to avoid injuries in the classroom.

- Do not play inside the classroom and do not throw things at others.
- Do not fight with your classmates. Do not hit or push them.
- Do not use sharp objects such as blades to sharpen your pencils. Use pencil sharpeners.
- Do not climb on desks or benches.

- Do not run or push others while climbing up or down the stairs.
- Stand in a queue and do not push one another while getting into or down from a school bus.

SAFETY ON THE ROAD

a

We should follow some safety rules to avoid injuries on the road.

- Always walk on the footpath or on the right side of the road facing the traffic.
- Do not play on the road.
- Cross the road only at the zebra crossing or use a subway[1].
- Before crossing the road, first look to your right and then to your left. When the road is clear or all the vehicles have stopped, only then cross the road.
- Never lean out of the window or door of a moving vehicle.
- Never stick out your head, hands and legs out from a moving vehicle.

Word Web

[1]**Subway:** an underground path

SAFETY IN THE PLAYGROUND

We should follow some safety rules to avoid injuries in the playground.

- Always wait for your turn on the swing. Do not stand in front of the swing. It might hit you.
- Do not push or pull one another while climbing the slide.
- Do not fight while playing.

Revise and Recall

Fill in the blanks using the correct words. ia

1. Do not play ________ games inside the house. (indoor/outdoor)
2. Use a ____________ to sharpen a pencil. (blade/sharpener)
3. _____ lean out of the window of a moving vehicle. (Always/Never)
4. Do not ____________ with your classmates. (fight/play)

FIRST AID

a

Even if we follow safety rules, sometimes accidents do take place. In such situations, immediate help and care should be given to the injured person.

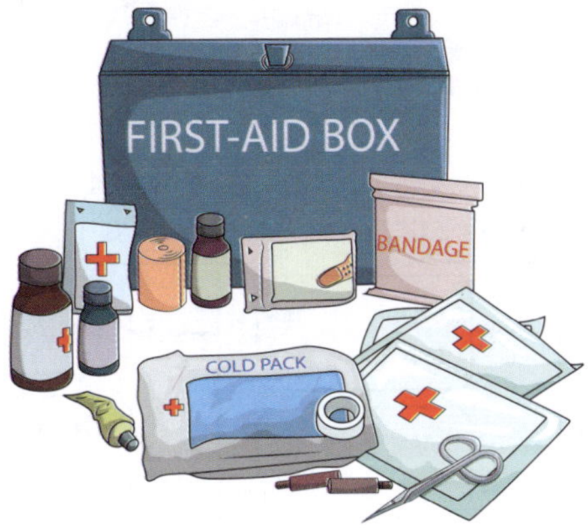

The immediate or first help given to an injured person before the doctor arrives is called **first aid**. A box that contains the things required to give first aid is called a **first-aid box**. It contains adhesive bandages, dressing material, scissors, antiseptic cream/lotion, cotton, etc.

If any of your friends gets hurt, you can take the following steps to give first aid:

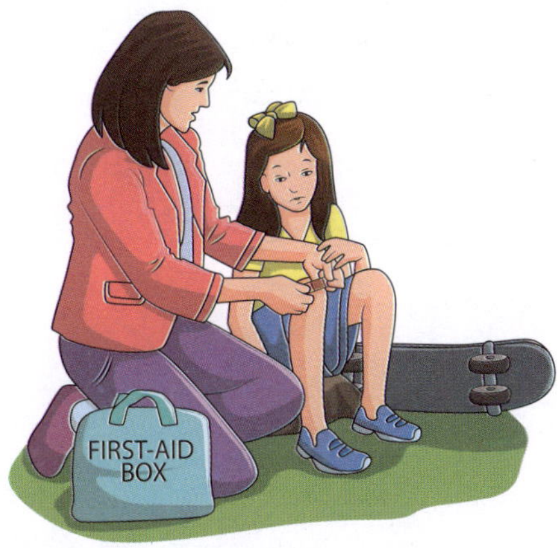

- Do not let other children crowd around the injured person.
- Keep the injured person calm and make him/her lie down.
- Give the person water to drink.
- In case of minor wounds, wash the area with running water. Wipe it and apply antiseptic cream/lotion.
  If there is loss of blood, tie a clean bandage or cloth.

Keywords

Safety: Staying away from harm or injury
First aid: The immediate or first help given to an injured person before the doctor arrives
First-aid box: A box that contains the things required to give first aid

Summary

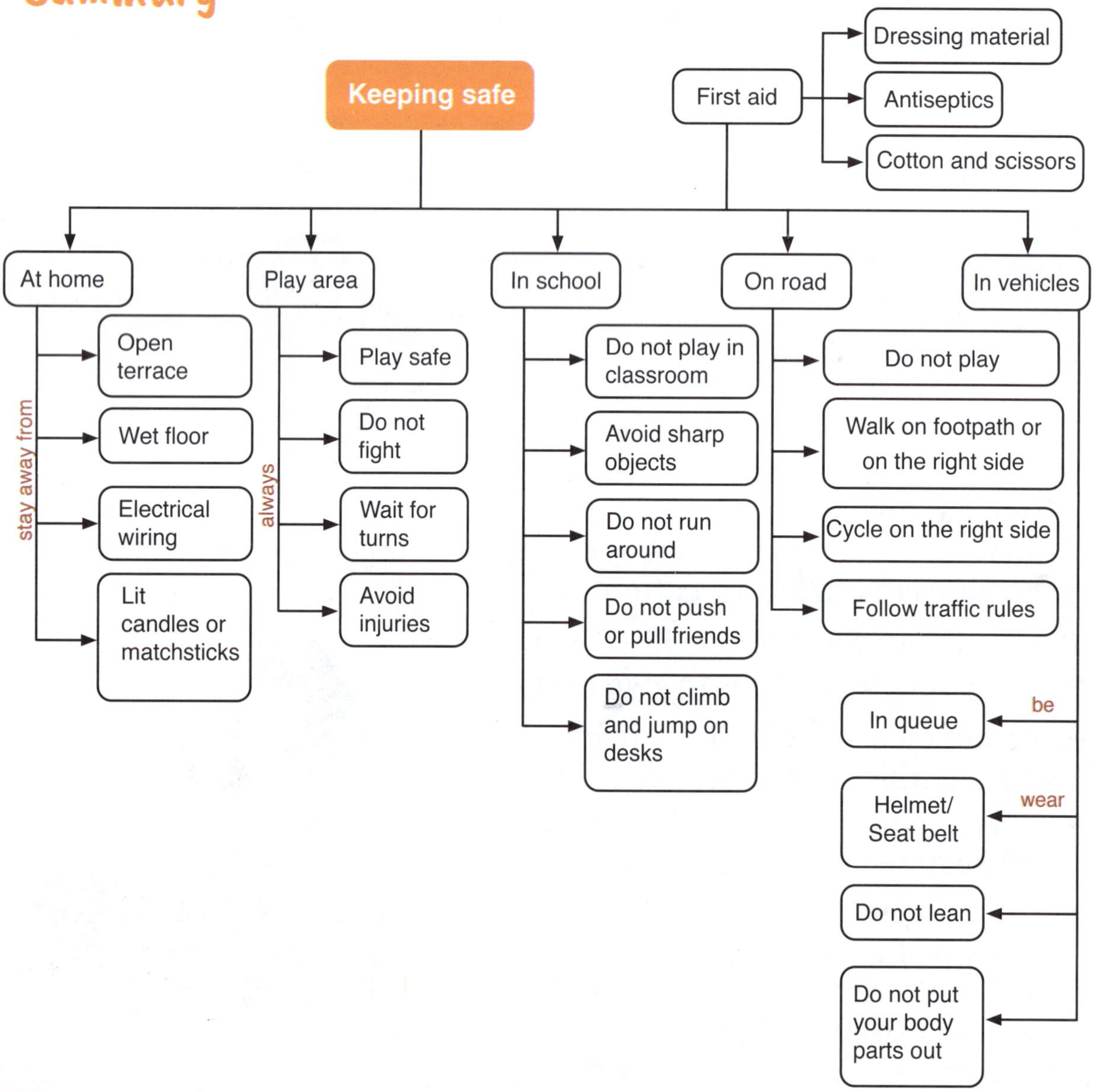

EXERCISE

W

A. Choose the correct option for each of the following.

ia

1. Which of the following can give you a cut?

   (a) Handkerchief (b) Knife (c) Eraser (d) Notebook

2. Which of the following should not be touched with wet hands?

   (a) Rubber ball (b) Toothbrush
   (c) Electric switches (d) Pencil

3. Which of the following should not be there in a first-aid box?

   (a) Bandage (b) Toys (c) Cotton (d) Scissors

B. Fill in the blanks using the correct words.

ia

1. Accidents can occur if we are not ____________. (careful/careless)
2. Always walk on the footpath or on the ____________ side of the road facing the traffic. (right/left)
3. Always ____________ for your turn on the swing. (wait/run)
4. The immediate help given to an injured person is called ____________. (operation/first aid)

C. Circle the odd one in each group.

ia

1. Switch, plug, wires, school bag
2. Scissors, bandage, playground, cotton
3. Traffic light, zebra crossing, subway, bandage
4. Blade, bench, knife, scissors

D. Match the following.

Column A	Column B
1. Sharpener	(a) First-aid box
2. Subway	(b) Pencils
3. Cotton	(c) Sharp object
4. Knife	(d) Underground path

E. Name the following.

ia

1. This happens when we are in a hurry and not careful __________
2. These should be followed to avoid accidents __________
3. The place where we should cross the road __________
4. The box that contains the things needed for first aid __________

F. Give reasons for the following.

1. We should not touch electrical switches, plugs or wires with wet hands.
2. Outdoor games should never be played inside the house or classroom.
3. We should never stand in front of a swing.
4. We should not wear synthetic clothes while lighting firecrackers.
5. We should not play with sharp objects such as scissors and knife.

G. Answer the following questions briefly.

1. Why do accidents take place?
2. List any two safety rules that should be followed at home.
3. What is first aid?
4. List any four items that should be there in a first-aid box.

H. Answer the following questions.

1. Write any four safety rules that should be followed in the classroom.
2. List any four safety rules that should be followed on the road.
3. What are the safety rules that we should follow in the playground?

COGNITIVE CORNER

Critical Thinking

Arun and Amit were walking together. Arun fell down and got hurt. It was a small wound. Think and write what first aid should be given to him.

Picture Study

In the picture given alongside, put a circle around the people who are not following safety rules on the road.

Project

Use coloured paper and cardboard to make a traffic signal. Display it in the class and discuss what each light stands for.

Life Skills

You have studied the safety rules to be followed on the road. Look at the following pictures and write 'yes' or 'no' against each question.

The bus has stopped. Is this the right place to cross the road?____________

There is no traffic here. Can we cross the road at this place? ____________

Can we cross here? ____________

Two cars are parked here. Can these boys stand and talk here? ____________

WORKSHEET

Most of the kitchens have either gas cylinders or piped gas for cooking. The name of this gas is liquified petroleum gas or LPG, in short.

This gas is used not only at homes, but also in roadside shops and restaurants. It burns cleanly without giving off any harmful gases.

However, it has to be used safely. In case gas leaks from either the cylinder or the pipes, it can cause fire.

The gas has no smell. It is colourless and cannot be seen. How can we know whether there is a gas leakage?

LPG cylinders

A foul-smelling gas is mixed with the cooking gas before delivering to our homes. In case the gas leaks, this smell alerts us.

Do not, under any circumstances, handle any electrical switch when you suspect gas leak. The gas might catch fire from a tiny spark. Do not light any matches or gas lighters. The gas may explode.

If you smell gas in your home, what should you do? Tick the correct responses.

1. Inform a grown-up immediately. ☐
2. There is no need to say anything, the smell will go away on its own. ☐
3. Try to light the burner to see whether gas is really leaking. ☐
4. Open all doors and windows. ☐
5. Turn the knob of the cylinder or pipe to 'off' position. ☐
6. Turn on the lights to see better. ☐
7. Do not touch any electrical switch. ☐
8. Leave the house till the situation is taken care of. ☐

7 Housing and Clothing

Learning Checklist
- Types of houses
- A good and clean house
- Clothes and fibres
- Clothes that suit the weather

Let's Get Started

Look at the pictures given below. These are the different rooms in a house. Write the name of each room with the help of the words given.

Kitchen	Bathroom	Bedroom	Drawing room

We need a house to live in. A house protects us from wind, heat, cold, rain, wild animals and thieves.

TYPES OF HOUSES

a

People live in different kinds of houses according to their needs. A house can be big or small, *kutcha* or *pucca*, temporary or permanent.

Kutcha House

A *kutcha* house is built with mud, straw and sticks. It can be easily destroyed by heavy rainfall or strong winds. A hut is an example of a *kutcha* house. *Kutcha* houses are mainly seen in the villages.

A hut

Pucca House

A *pucca* house is built with stones, cement, rods and bricks. It is a strong house and can withstand[1] harsh weather. Buildings, bungalows, cottages and apartments are examples of *pucca* houses.

A bungalow

A cottage

Word Web

[1]**Withstand:** to bear or cope with

Temporary Houses

People who keep moving from place to place use temporary houses to live in. Caravan, tent and yurt are some examples of temporary houses.

A caravan

A tent

A yurt

Permanent Houses

People who live at the same place for a long time live in permanent houses. Apartment, cottage and bungalow are some examples of permanent houses.

A GOOD AND CLEAN HOUSE

a

Whether big or small, a house should be clean and airy.

A good house should get plenty of fresh air and sunlight.

All the rooms in a house should have doors and windows to let in sunlight and fresh air. Sunlight keeps the room free from germs.

Windows let in sunlight and fresh air

Wire netting should be fixed on the window frames and doors to keep the flies and mosquitoes away. They also allow sunlight and air to come in.

There should be an open space such as a veranda or courtyard. This provides a place for children to play and for others to enjoy fresh air.

Wire netting on window

A courtyard

Keeping the House Clean

To stay healthy, we should always keep our house and its surroundings clean. The house should always be kept free from dust and germs.

Some ways to keep the house clean are given below:

- All the objects should be kept in their proper places.
- The floor should be swept and mopped every day.
- The kitchen should be cleaned regularly and the food should be kept covered.
- The doors, windows and the furniture should be dusted regularly. There should be curtains for doors and windows to keep dust away.
- The washbasins, bathrooms and toilets should be cleaned daily.
- Household wastes should be thrown inside dustbins. Dustbins should be kept covered to keep away houseflies and mosquitoes.
- If there are pets at home, their living place should be cleaned regularly.

Go Green

Plants and trees should be grown around the house to keep the environment green and fresh.

Revise and Recall

Fill in the blanks using the correct words. ia

1. A good house should be airy and __________. (dark/well-lit)
2. The windows of the house should be kept __________ to let the fresh air in. (closed/open)
3. Household wastes should be thrown __________ the dustbins. (inside/outside)

CLOTHES AND FIBRES

We wear clothes to protect our body from the sun's heat, rain, cold, dust and insects. Clothes are made up of very fine threads called **fibres**. Fibres can be natural or man-made.

Natural Fibres

Fibres obtained from plants and animals are called **natural fibres**. Examples of natural fibres are cotton, jute, wool, flax and silk.

Science in Context

Clothes can be made from bamboo and hemp fibres also.

Fibres obtained from plants

Cotton fibre is obtained from the cotton plant. It is used to make cotton clothes such as saree, shirt, trousers and skirt.

Jute fibre is obtained from the jute plant. It is used to make clothes and other items such as bag, mat and rope.

Cotton plant

Cotton fibre

Cotton dress

Jute plant

Jute fibre

Jute bag

Fibres obtained from animals

We get wool from sheep. Wool is used to make woollen clothes. Fur of some animals such as silver fox is used to make warm clothing such as coats and sweaters.

We get silk from silkworm. The silkworm weaves a cocoon around it. The silk thread is obtained from the cocoon. Silk threads are woven into sarees and scarves.

Sheep

Wool

Woollen sweater

Silkworms and silk cocoon

Silk threads

Silk saree

Science in Context

Silkworms eat the leaves of mulberry plant. The rearing of silkworms for the production of silk is called **sericulture**.

Man-made Fibres

Fibres manufactured by human beings are called man-made fibres. Man-made fibres are also called **synthetic fibres**. Examples of man-made fibres are polyester and nylon.

Polyester leggings

Nylon rope

CLOTHES THAT SUIT THE WEATHER

The type of clothes we wear depends on the weather.

In hot or warm weather, people mostly wear light-coloured cotton clothes. Cotton clothes absorb sweat and keep the body cool. Light-coloured clothes absorb very little heat of the sun and keep the body cool.

Summer clothes

Winter clothes

In cold weather, people wear dark-coloured woollen clothes.

Woollen clothes keep the body warm by not letting the body heat escape. Dark-coloured clothes absorb the sun's heat and keep the body warm.

People living in very cold and snowy places wear clothes made of fur[1] to keep themselves warm.

Word Web

[1]**Fur**: the thick hair that grows on the bodies of many animals

Clothes for rainy weather

During rainy season, we wear raincoats and carry umbrellas to protect ourselves from the rain. Raincoats and umbrellas are made up of rubber or plastic. Plastic and rubber are a waterproof materials which do not absorb water.

Keywords

Fibres: Very fine threads used to make clothes

***Kutcha* house:** A house built with mud, straw and sticks

***Pucca* house:** A house built with stones, cement, rods and bricks

Natural fibres: Fibres that are obtained from plants and animals

Man-made/synthetic fibres: Fibres that are made by human beings

Summary

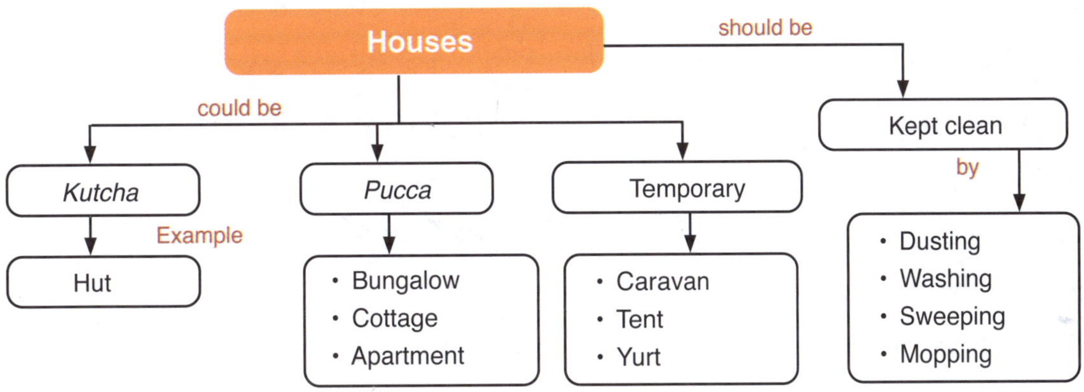

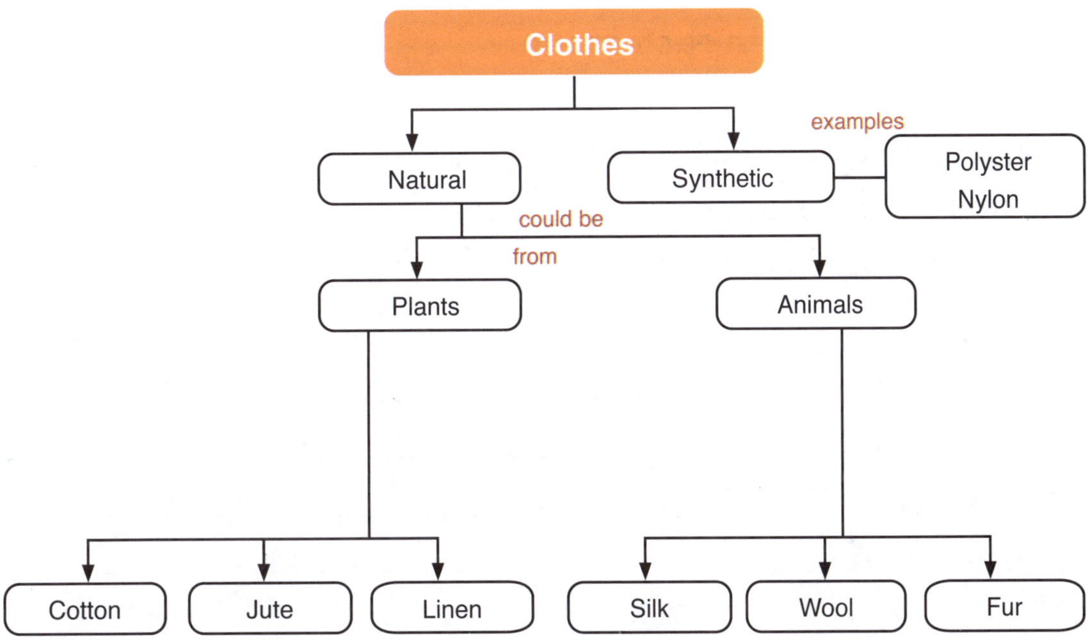

EXERCISE

W

A. Fill in the blanks using the correct words.

1. A good house should get plenty of fresh air and __________. (sunlight/water)
2. All the objects in the house should be kept at __________ places. (any/proper)
3. Natural fibres are obtained from plants and __________. (animals/insects)
4. The fibre obtained from __________ is an animal fibre. (jute/sheep)
5. Woollen clothes protect our body from __________ and keep us warm. (heat/cold)

B. Match the following.

	Column A		Column B
1.	Cotton	(a)	Silk
2.	Wool	(b)	Raincoat
3.	Umbrella	(c)	Shirt
4.	Rubber	(d)	During rains
5.	Cocoons	(e)	Sheep

C. Circle the odd one in each group.

ia

1. Cotton, wool, jute
2. Silk, raincoat, umbrella
3. Sweater, woollen gloves, cotton shirt
4. Silkworm, cocoon, bamboo

D. Give two examples for each of the following.

1. Permanent house __________ and __________
2. Natural fibre __________ and __________
3. Things made of jute __________ and __________
4. Things made of silk __________ and __________

E. Give reasons for the following.

1. In cold weather, people wear dark-coloured woollen clothes.
2. Raincoats and umbrellas are made of rubber or plastic material.
3. Cotton is a natural fibre.
4. There should be an open space such as a veranda or courtyard in a house.
5. Wire netting should be fixed on the window frames and doors.

F. Answer the following questions briefly.

1. Write any two ways to keep your house clean.
2. What do clothes protect us from?
3. What is a fibre?

G. Answer the following questions.

1. What are the features of a good and clean house?
2. Describe the different kinds of fibres with examples.
3. How is silk produced?

COGNITIVE CORNER

Critical Thinking

Anshu is going for a trip to Rajasthan in April. Her father asked her to keep light-coloured cotton clothes. Why?

Picture Study

For the pictures given below, write the name of the fibre and one object made from each. One has been done for you.

Jute plant

Jute fibre

Jute bag

Wool

____

____

Cotton plant

____

____

Silkworm and cocoon

____

____

Project

Make the model of a hut using popsicle sticks.

Materials required:
Popsicle sticks and glue

Set 10 popsicle sticks side by side and stick them by applying glue. The back wall of the hut is ready. In the same way, make the side walls. Glue along the sides of both the corners and let it dry. To make the front side of the hut, set only seven popsicle sticks and leave the rest open for the entrance of the hut. Similarly, make two sets of walls for the roof. You can also colour the sticks.

Life Skills

Number the pictures to match them with the statements given below.

 ◯  ◯  ◯  ◯

1. Always throw waste paper or any other waste in the dustbin.
2. After studying, arrange your books neatly on the bookshelf.
3. Do not throw your toys around. Keep them in their proper places.
4. Do not spill food on the table while eating. Spread a napkin on your lap before you start to eat.

WORKSHEET

We wear clothes according to the season. In winters we wear woollen clothes, during rainy season we wear raincoats. Have you wondered how animals cope with such weather changes?

We have seen birds swimming in water. After staying for such a long time in water, don't the swans, ducks and other birds catch cold? Just as we wear raincoats, they too have a system which protects their skin from getting wet.

Swan in water

Swan preening

They have a layer of smooth feathers which acts like their raincoat. Also, their skin secretes oil.

You might have seen water birds running their beaks through their feathers. This is called preening. They do so to coat the oil on the feathers. The layer of oil prevents water from wetting their bodies.

Deserts are usually very hot. Animals that live in deserts such as camels have thick skin and less hair on their body. This helps to prevent water loss from their body.

Camel

Find out how the following animals protect themselves from extreme cold in polar regions.

Penguin

Polar bear

8 Air, Water and Weather

Learning Checklist

- What is air made up of?
- Water
- Weather
- Seasons

Let's Get Started

Look at the pictures given below and fill in the blanks.

The boy is blowing ________ into the balloon.

________ is helping the kite to fly.

The girl is breathing in ________ .

Air is essential for all living things. Let us learn what air contains and read about the water cycle and weather.

WHAT IS AIR MADE UP OF?

Gases: Air is made up of gases such as nitrogen, oxygen and carbon dioxide. We breathe in oxygen and breathe out carbon dioxide. Oxygen is also required for burning things. Nitrogen is important for the growth of plants.

Science in Context

Deep-sea divers carry oxygen cylinders for breathing underwater.

Water vapour: Have you ever seen wet clothes hung out to dry on a clothesline? What happens to them after a while? They dry up. Where does the water from the clothes vanish? The heat of the sun changes the water into water vapour. This vapour gets mixed with the air around. Hence, air contains water vapour.

Clothes drying in the sun

Dust particles: If you carefully observe a beam of light entering a dark room, you will see small particles floating in the light. These are dust particles. Thus, air also contains dust particles.

Smoke and germs: When we burn something, it gives out smoke. Vehicles also give out smoke. All this smoke gets mixed with the air. When we sneeze or cough, we release germs into the air. Thus, air also contains smoke and germs.

WATER

a

All living beings need water to live. We use water in many ways. We use it for drinking, washing, cooking, bathing, etc. but still there is enough supply of water on the Earth. How does this happen? This is because there is continuous movement of water between the land, water bodies and the air. There are two processes involved in this movement of water—evaporation and condensation.

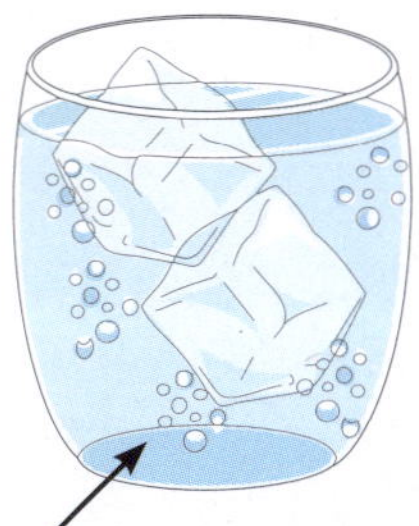

Evaporation is the process in which water changes into water vapour. When wet clothes dry, water changes into water vapour.

Condensation is the process in which water vapour changes into water. You must have seen that small water droplets form on the outer surface of a cold drink bottle or a glass with cold water.

Both evaporation and condensation are continuous processes occurring in nature.

Water Cycle

a

Due to the sun's heat, water gets heated and evaporates from seas, rivers, lakes and ponds as water vapour. Water vapour rises up into the air. After reaching a great height, water vapour condenses into tiny droplets of water. These water droplets join together to form bigger drops, which in turn join to form clouds. When clouds become heavy with water drops, the water drops fall on the surface of the Earth as rain. Some part of the rainwater seeps into the soil and gets collected underground.

The continuous movement of water between the land, water bodies and air is called the **water cycle**.

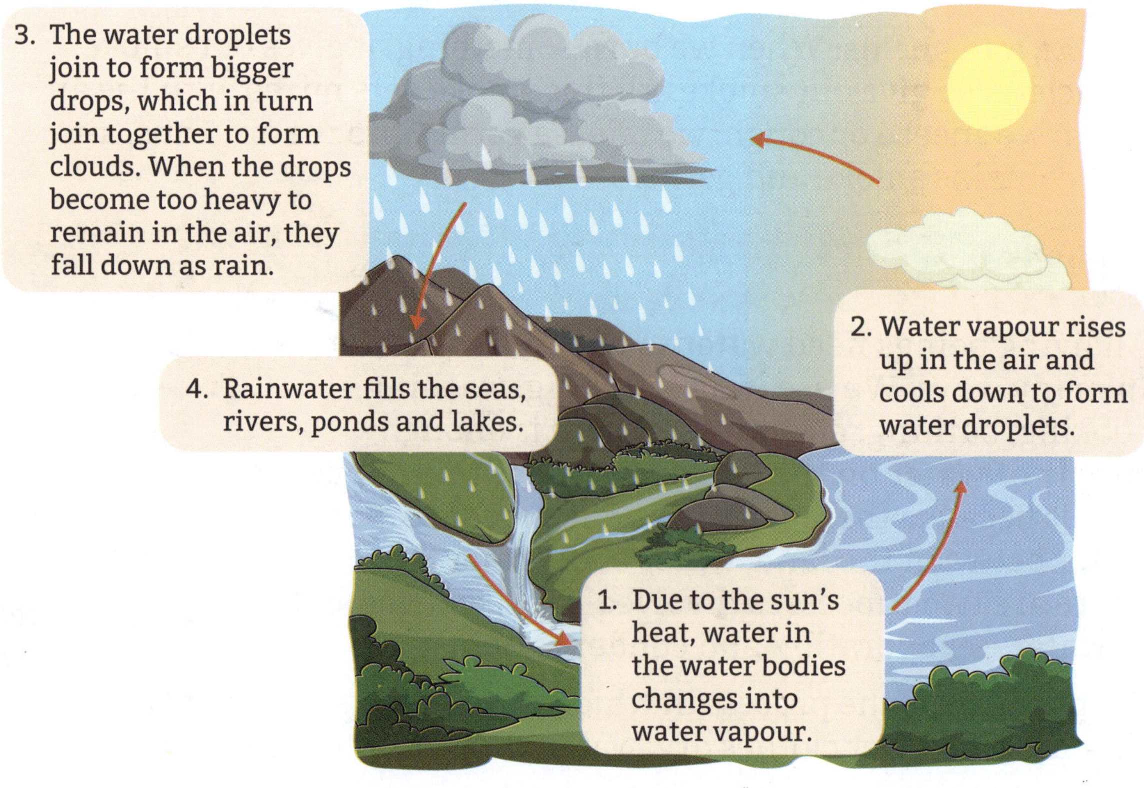

Water cycle

Revise and Recall

Fill in the blanks using the correct words. ia

1. When we sneeze or cough, __________ get released into the air. (smoke/germs)
2. Heat from the __________ evaporates water in seas, rivers, lakes and ponds. (moon/sun)
3. The cool air changes water vapour into tiny droplets of __________. (cloud/water)
4. Water drops fall on the surface of the Earth as __________. (water vapour/rain)

WEATHER

a

Weather is the day-to-day condition of a particular place. It depends on the sun, wind, clouds and water vapour in the air. The clothes we wear, the food we eat and the things we do, all depend on the weather.

Following are the different types of weather that we experience.

A hot day

Hot Weather

When the sun shines very brightly, the day becomes hot. We sweat more, feel thirsty and drink a lot of water. We wear light cotton clothes on a hot day because cotton clothes help our body to stay cool. We like to take cold drinks on hot days.

Cold Weather

The sun is hidden behind the clouds on a cold day. We wear woollen clothes in cold weather. We drink hot tea or soup and prefer to stay inside our houses.

A cold day

Cloudy Weather

The clouds gather up and cover the rays of the sun and bring shade on the Earth. Such weather is called cloudy weather. When the clouds are thick and grey, they bring rain.

Cloudy weather

Windy Weather

We know that moving air is called wind. We can notice wind by feeling, hearing and seeing its effect on the things around us. When the wind blows gently, it is called **breeze**. A strong wind is called **gale**. When the wind becomes so strong that it can cause damage by uprooting trees and houses, we call it **storm**.

Breeze

Gale

Storm

Rainy Weather

When it rains, we call it a rainy day.

Our surroundings get wet and the rain cools down the part of the Earth where it falls.

Crops grow well if it rains at the right time. People use umbrellas, and wear raincoats and gumboots when they go out in the rain.

A rainy day

SEASONS

Change of weather after every few months brings different seasons. Summer, winter, monsoon, autumn and spring are the five main seasons.

It is very hot during summers; hot winds blow during this time. Winters are very cold. Places that have extremely cold weather receive snowfall. It rains heavily during the monsoon season. Trees shed their leaves during autumn. During spring, the flowers are in full bloom.

Summer

Winter

Monsoon

Autumn

Spring

Keywords

Evaporation: The process in which water changes into water vapour

Condensation: The process in which water vapour changes into water

Water cycle: The continous movement of water between the land, water bodies and air

Weather: The day-to-day condition of a particular place

Season: The change of weather after every few months results in seasons

Summary

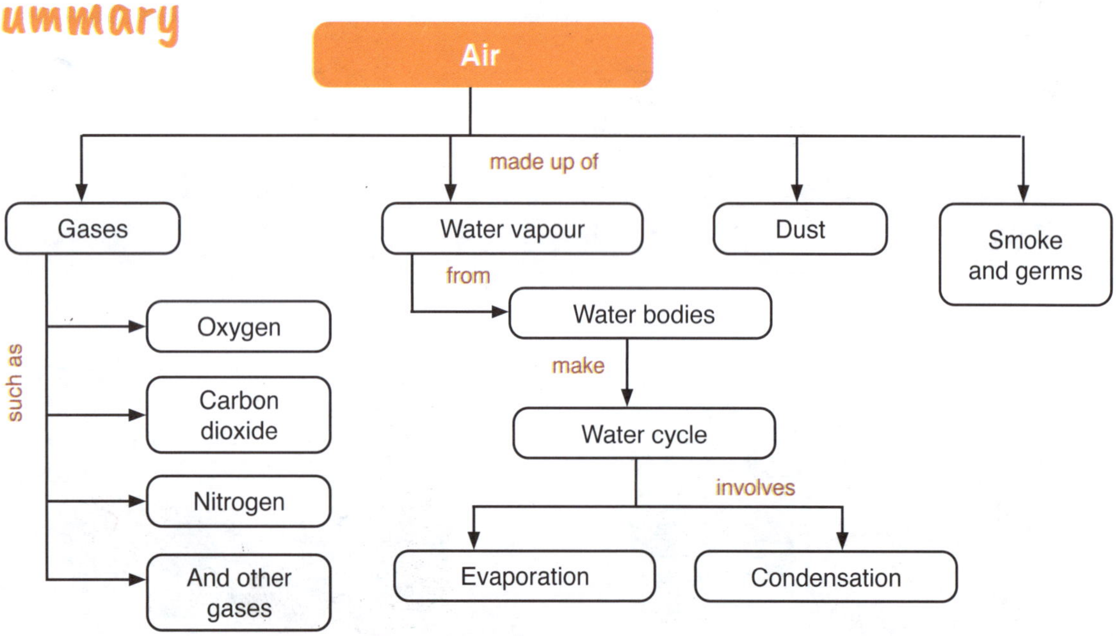

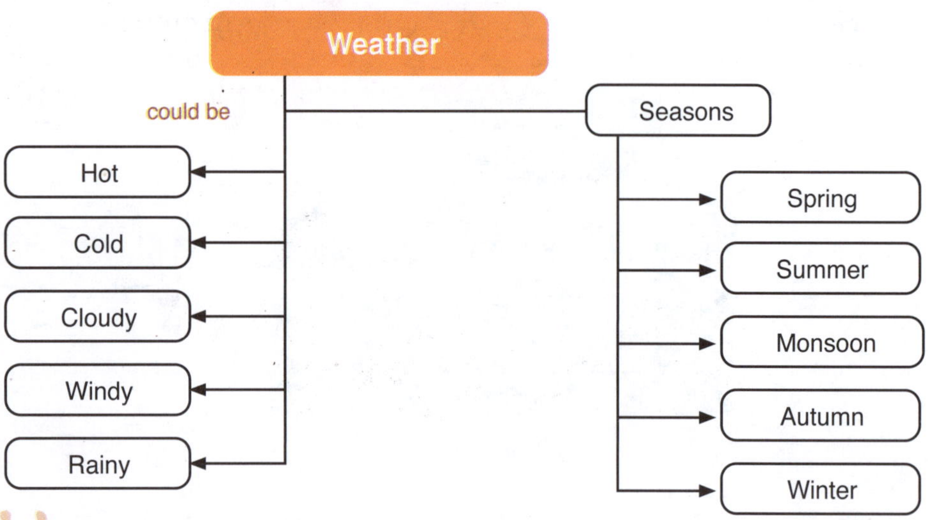

EXERCISE

W

A. Choose the correct answer for each of the following.

ia

1. This gas is required for burning.
   (a) Nitrogen (b) Oxygen
   (c) Both of these (d) None of these
2. Air contains __________ .
   (a) gases (b) water vapour
   (c) dust (d) all of these
3. __________ is the process in which water vapour changes into water.
   (a) Evaporation (b) Boiling
   (c) Condensation (d) Freezing
4. When the wind blows gently, it is called a __________ .
   (a) breeze (b) storm
   (c) gale (d) none of these

B. Fill in the blanks with the correct words.

ia

1. Water is present in the air in the form of __________ . (ice/water vapour)
2. We often feel thirsty during __________ days. (rainy/hot)
3. Moving air is called __________ . (cloud/wind)
4. Trees shed their leaves during __________ . (spring/autumn)

C. State whether the following statements are true (T) or false (F).

1. Air is important for all living things. ☐
2. Nitrogen is important for the growth of plants. ☐
3. Air contains dust particles. ☐
4. Evaporation is the process in which water turns into ice. ☐
5. Weather is the same in all parts of the world. ☐

D. **Match the following.**

Column A	Column B
1. Umbrellas and raincoats	(a) Gale
2. Clouds gather up	(b) Rainy day
3. Sun shines brightly	(c) Cloudy day
4. Strong wind	(d) Sunny day

E. **Name the following.** ia

1. The process in which water vapour changes into water ____________
2. The day-to-day condition of a particular place ____________
3. The strong wind that can cause damage to houses and trees ____________
4. The change of weather after every few months ____________

F. **Give reasons for the following.**

1. Water cycle is a continuous process.
2. Water droplets are seen on the outer surface of a cold object.
3. The wet clothes hung on a clotheslines dry up after a while.
4. Deep sea divers carry oxygen cylinders.
5. We drink soup on a cold day.

G. **Answer the following questions briefly.**

1. What does air contain?
2. What is the difference between breeze and gale?
3. What are the different types of weather?

H. **Answer the following questions.**

1. Explain the water cycle.
2. How does weather affect our daily life? Explain.
3. What are the five main seasons? Write one sentence about what happens in each season.

COGNITIVE CORNER

Critical Thinking

1. Cloudy days are cooler than sunny days. Why?
2. We wear light-coloured clothes on sunny days. Why?

Picture Study

Label the water cycle diagram using the following words.

- Condensation
- Evaporation
- Sun
- Rain

Project

Have you ever seen weather reports on TV? There are different symbols used to indicate different types of weather. Given below are a few weather symbols. What do these weather symbols represent? Find out and collect/draw other symbols used in weather reports. How is it different from the symbols used in newspapers? Make a chart or a report based on your findings.

Life Skills

When it rains, our surroundings get wet. Sometimes, it rains heavily and causes many problems. Have you faced any problems due to rains? How can you help people who face problems during heavy rains?

9 INDUSTRY, INNOVATION AND INFRASTRUCTURE

WORKSHEET

You read about the water cycle in this chapter. Water evaporates from water bodies and forms clouds. These clouds in turn give us rain and snow. The extra water flows back into the water bodies, thus completing the cycle.

Let us try to create a water cycle of our own. You must remember to take the help of an adult to do this experiment.

What we need:

- A gas stove
- A kettle
- A flat plate
- Water
- Tongs
- Container

We can now start making our own water cycle.

1. Request the adult who is helping you to put the kettle on a gas stove. Add some water in it.
2. When the water starts boiling, request them to hold the plate over the steam coming out from the kettle.
3. You will see that drops of water appear on the plate where the steam touches it.
4. Take a container and request your helper to tilt the plate.
5. You can collect the water in the container.

You have successfully created a water cycle at your home!

Fill the following table. Record what you know, wonder, and learnt about water cycle.

Know What I Know	Wonder What I Wonder	Learnt What I Learnt

9 Sun, Moon and Stars

Learning Checklist

- Sun and the solar system
- Moon
- Stars

Let's Get Started

You have already learnt about some of the objects seen in the morning and night sky in Class 1. Let us see if you can identify them.

Fill in the blanks with the help of the pictures given below.

The ________ is visible in the sky during the day.

The ________ is visible as a white ball at night.

________ can be seen twinkling in the night sky.

Let us learn more about the sun, moon and stars.

SUN AND THE SOLAR SYSTEM

a

We can see the sun in the sky during the day. It gives us heat and light. It is a big ball of fire very far away from the Earth.

The **solar system** is made up of the sun and the eight planets. **Planets** are huge round objects that move around the sun in fixed paths called **orbits**. Planets do not have light of their own and reflect the light of the sun that falls on them.

The sun is at the centre of the solar system. The eight planets moving around the sun are Mercury, Venus, Earth, Mars, Jupiter, Saturn, Uranus and Neptune.

① **Mercury** is the smallest and the closest planet to the sun.

② **Venus** is the brightest as well as the hottest planet. It is also called the evening star or the morning star.

③ Our **Earth** is the third planet from the sun. It is the only planet where life is known to exist.

Solar system (not to scale)

④ **Mars** is known as the red planet because of its red colour.

⑤ **Jupiter** is the largest planet in the solar system.

⑥ **Saturn** is the lightest among all the planets and has rings around it.

⑦ **Uranus** is the seventh planet from the sun.

⑧ **Neptune** is the farthest planet from the sun. It is blue in colour.

Science in Context

- Mercury, Venus, Earth and Mars are made up of rocks and metals.
- Jupiter and Saturn are made up of gases.
- Uranus and Neptune are made up of ice and gases.

MOON

a

The moon is the natural **satellite** of the Earth. A satellite is an object that moves continuously around a planet. The moon takes 27 days to go around the Earth once. It is smaller than the Earth and can be seen with the naked eye. The moon is seen at night. It does not have any light of its own. It reflects the light of the sun.

Moon

The moon can be seen clearly with the help of a telescope. **Telescope** is an instrument that helps us to see faraway objects closely and clearly. When seen through a telescope, a lot of large pits are seen on the surface of the moon. These pits are called **craters**. There is no air on the moon and it has a lot of mountains and valleys.

Looking through a telescope

The moon seen through a telescope

Neil Armstrong, in the year 1969, became the first human to have landed and walked on the moon.

We do not get to see the moon as a complete circle every time we look at the night sky. At times, we see a half-moon, at times less than half, sometimes full and at times we cannot see the moon at all. The different shapes of the moon that we see are called the **phases of the moon**.

New moon Half-moon Full moon

Phases of the moon

Science in Context

- From the Earth, we always see the same side of the moon, the other side is always hidden.
- Except Mercury and Venus, all the other planets have natural satellites moving around them.

Revise and Recall

Fill in the blanks using the correct words.

1. ________ are huge round objects that move around the sun through their orbits. (Stars/Planets)
2. The ________ is at the centre of the solar system. (Earth/sun)
3. ________ is the largest planet in the solar system. (Jupiter/Earth)
4. The moon is an example for _______. (planet/satellite)
5. The moon takes ______ days to go around the Earth once. (27/24)

STARS

Stars are huge balls of fire, which produce heat and light. The sun is also a star. Stars are very far away from us and hence appear as dots of light in the night sky. The sun appears bigger in size as it is nearer to the Earth than the other stars. Some stars appear brighter than the others.

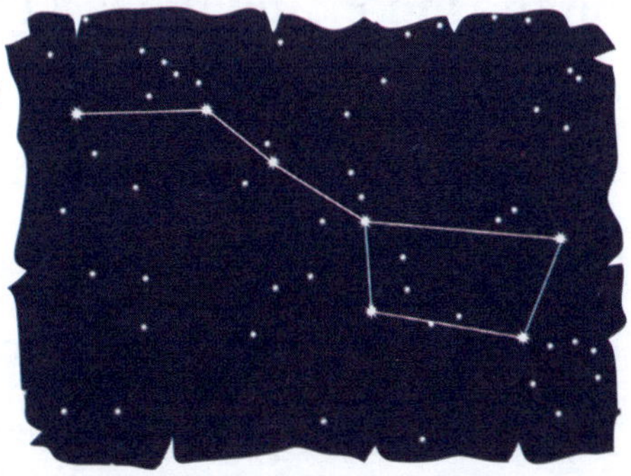

Ursa Major (Great Bear)

Orion (Hunter)

Stars can be seen through the naked eye and also with the help of a telescope.

A group of stars forming a certain pattern in the night sky is called **constellation**.

Each constellation is given a name based on human imagination. Some of the easily seen constellations are Ursa Major (Great Bear) and Orion (Hunter). All constellations cannot be seen at all times. They appear according to the seasons.

Keywords

Planets: Huge round objects which move around the sun in their own fixed paths

Orbit: The fixed path taken by planets to move around the sun

Satellite: An object that continuously moves around a planet

Telescope: An instrument that helps us to see faraway objects closely and clearly

Craters: Large pits on the surface of the moon

Constellation: A group of stars forming a certain pattern in the night sky

Summary

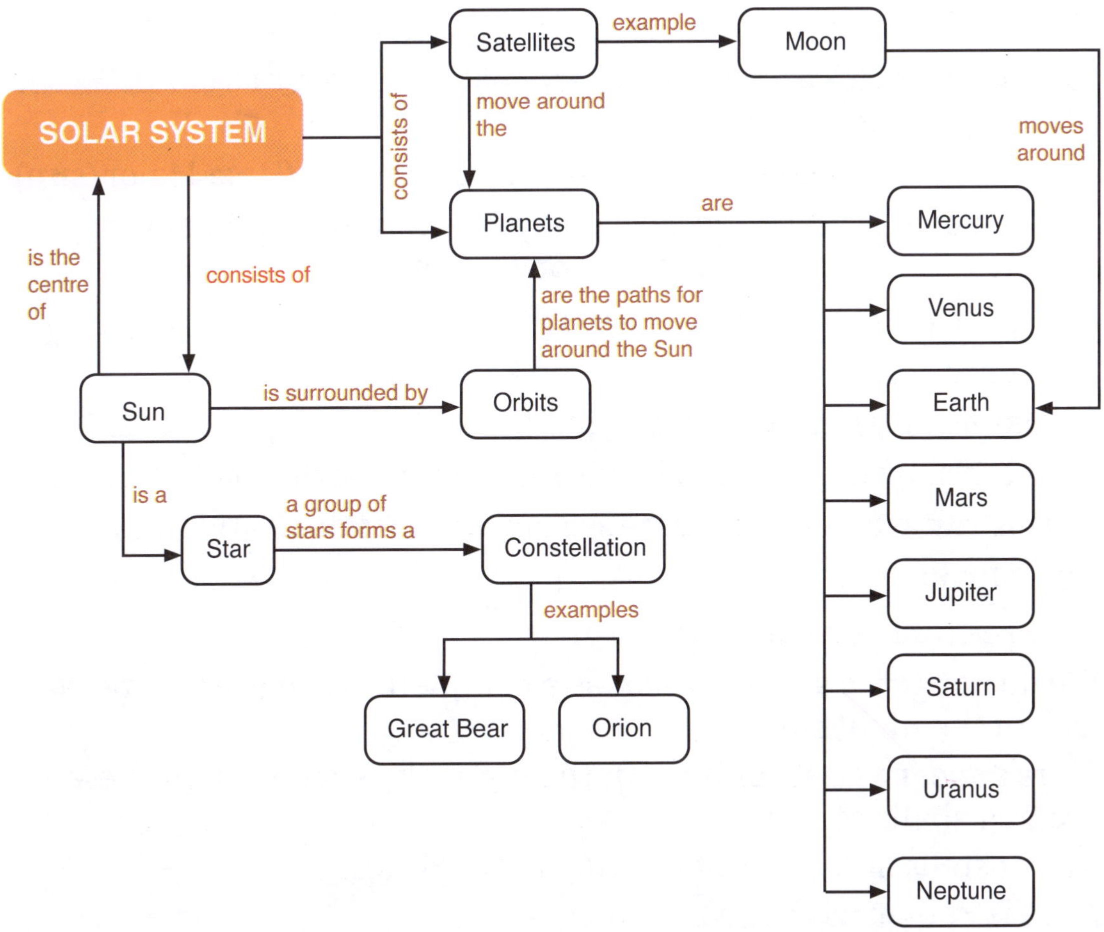

EXERCISE

W

A. Choose the correct option for each of the following.

1. Which among the following is a planet?
   (a) Sun (b) Moon (c) Jupiter (d) Orion
2. Which one of the following provides light and heat?
   (a) Moon (b) Jupiter (c) Saturn (d) Sun
3. The planet that is the farthest from the sun is
   (a) Neptune (b) Uranus (c) Saturn (d) Earth
4. The natural satellite of the Earth is the
   (a) Mars (b) Mercury (c) Moon (d) Venus
5. Identify a constellation.
   (a) Crater (b) Orion (c) Mercury (d) Mars

B. Fill in the blanks with the correct words. ia

1. The Earth is the ____________ planet from the sun. (third/fourth)
2. The moon has no ____________. (mountains/air)
3. Faraway objects can be seen clearly with the help of a ____________. (naked eye/telescope)
4. The closest star to the Earth is the ____________. (Ursa Major/sun)
5. A group of stars forming a certain pattern in the night sky is called ____________. (constellation/crater)

C. Answer the following in one word each. ia

1. The source of light and heat on the Earth ____________
2. The largest planet moving around the sun ____________
3. Days taken by the moon to move around the Earth once ____________
4. The instrument that helps us to see faraway objects clearly ____________
5. Any constellation ____________

D. Give reasons for the following.

1. We do not get to see the moon as a complete circle every time we look at the night sky.
2. Stars appear as dots of light in the night sky even though these are huge balls of fire.
3. All constellations cannot be seen all the times.
4. Mars is known as the red planet.

E. Answer the following questions briefly.

1. What is an orbit?
2. What is a satellite?
3. What are craters?
4. Why does the sun appear to be bigger in size than the rest of the stars?

F. Answer the following questions.

1. What are the features of planets? Name all the planets in increasing order of distance from the sun.
2. Write a short note on the solar system.
3. What are the phases of the moon?
4. What are stars?
5. How are constellations named? Name two constellations that can be easily seen in the night sky.

COGNITIVE CORNER

Critical Thinking

Why are the stars and the moon visible only at night and not during the day?

Picture Study

Identify the planets and write their names.

__________ __________ __________

Project

Take a black chart paper and make a night sky on the same. Show stars, moon and a constellation. Use silver paper to show the moon.

Life Skills

The sun is the only natural source of heat and light to us. List out at least two ways in which you can make use of the heat and light in your life.

WORKSHEET

The planet Earth belongs to a family called the solar system. The eight planets revolve around a star called the sun. The sun is the most important member of this family. Early Man regarded the sun as a god.

Sun

A. Write down the two most important things we get from the sun.

1. ______________________

2. ______________________

Earth is the only planet in the solar system to have life. All the animals depends directly or indirectly on plants. Plants need energy from the sun to prepare food.

B. Fill in the blanks using the correct words.

Sun	Rain	Clouds	Sea

Rivers and ponds get water from ____________. We get it from ____________ which are formed when water evaporates from the ____________ due to heating effect of ____________.

Sun is what makes the water cycle work.

C. What would happen if sun was removed from the water cycle? Give reason for your answers.

____

____

____

____

____

10 Our Earth

Learning Checklist

- Life on Earth
- Shape of the Earth
- Movements of the Earth
- Human beings and Earth

Let's Get Started

In Chapter 8, you have learned about different seasons.

Look at the given pictures and fill in the blanks to know the seasons on the Earth.

When does it snow?

W _ N T _ _

When will it be sunny?

S U _ _ E _

When does it rain?

M _ N S _ _ N

Different seasons on the Earth occur due to the movement of the Earth around the sun.

In this chapter, let us study more about the shape and movements of the Earth.

LIFE ON EARTH

When the Earth was formed, it was very hot. The hot water vapour released from it cooled down, formed clouds and poured down as rain. This cooled down the surface of the Earth. Slowly living things began to appear on the Earth. The Earth is the only planet where life is known to exist.

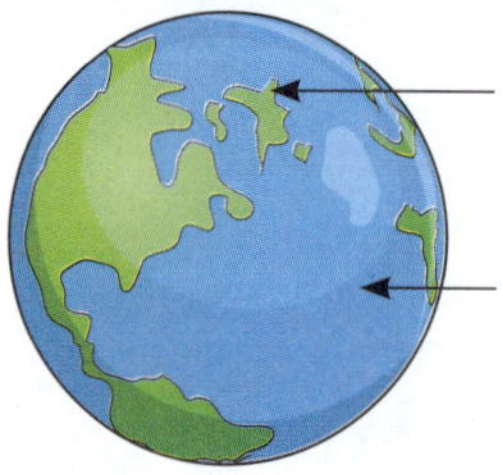

Our Earth

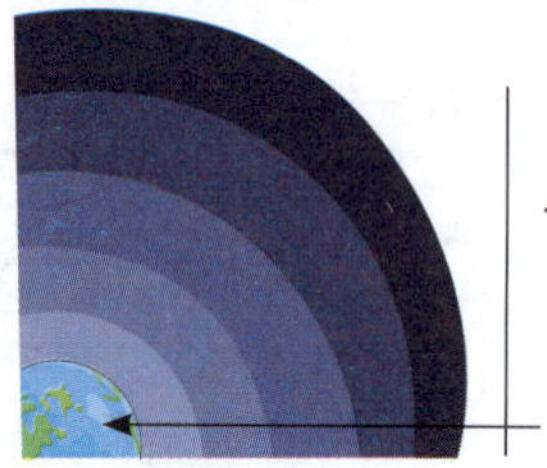

Atmosphere around the Earth

The Earth has land, water and air, which are the three main features that support life on this planet. Air covers the entire Earth like a blanket. This blanket of air around the Earth is called the **atmosphere**. All living beings need air to breathe.

Different living beings on the Earth

We live on land and it makes up one-fourth of the Earth. The remaining three-fourths of the Earth is covered with water. This is the reason why the Earth looks blue from outer space. Water is necessary for all living things.

We get light from the sun that helps plants and animals to grow. The heat from the sun keeps the Earth warm and hence, it supports life on this planet.

SHAPE OF THE EARTH

Long time ago, people believed that the Earth was flat. They believed that the sea would end in a drop and it was a point of no return. People did not travel much by sea.

A photograph taken from the moon shows the Earth as a sphere

We now know that the Earth is not flat. The satellite images of the Earth taken from space show that the Earth is round in shape. The photographs taken from the moon also clearly show that the Earth is like a huge blue ball.

This can be understood by making an observation. When you visit the seashore and see ships sailing on the sea, keep on observing a ship until it is far away from you. You will see that even after the lower part of the ship goes out of your sight, the upper part will be visible to you. If the Earth were flat, the whole ship would have been out of your sight.

View of the ship if the Earth was flat

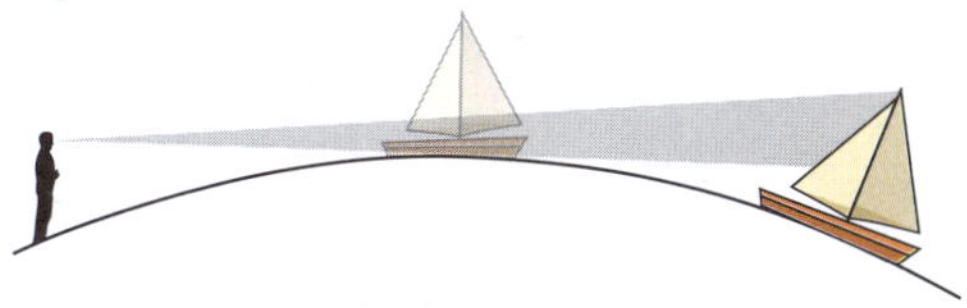

Actual view of the ship that proves the Earth is round

Science in Context

Ferdinand Magellan was a Portuguese explorer who organized a trip to go around the Earth through the sea. The time of their journey was from 1519 to 1522. They started from a port in Seville, Spain, and returned to the port after going around the Earth through the sea. This proved that the Earth is spherical in shape.

Revise and Recall

Fill in the blanks with the correct words.

1. The blanket of air around the Earth is called the ______________. (atmosphere/weather)
2. We live on the planet ______________. (Mars/Earth)
3. During the day, we get light from the ______________. (moon/sun)
4. Land makes up ______________ of the Earth. (three-fourths/one-fourth)

MOVEMENTS OF THE EARTH

The Earth is spherical in shape and is not stationary[1]. It shows two types of movements—rotation and revolution.

Word Web

[1]**Stationary:** resting

Rotation

When you play with a top, it spins on a point in a vertical line that passes through its centre. This fixed line is imaginary and is called the **axis** of movement. In a similar way, the Earth spins on an axis. The two opposite points on the Earth's surface through which the axis passes are called the **poles**. The Earth has two poles—the North Pole and the South Pole.

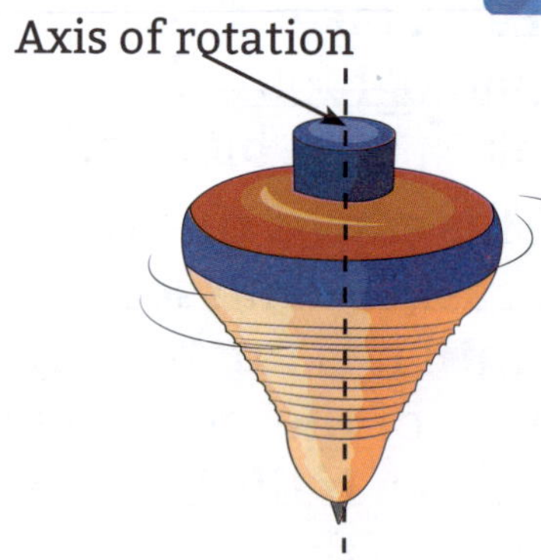

Spinning top

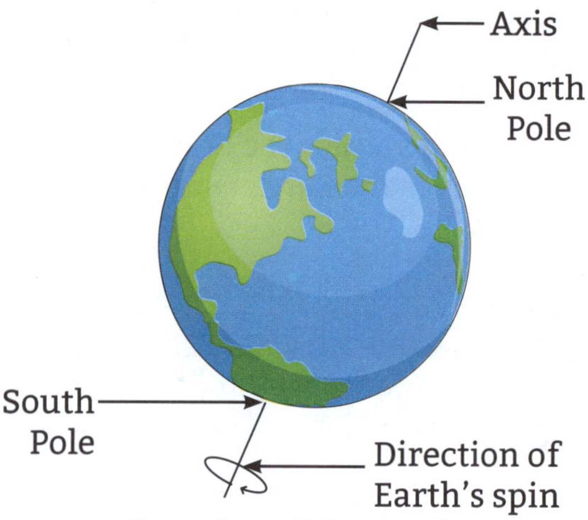

Rotation of the Earth

The movement of the Earth on its own axis is called **rotation**. The axis of the Earth is not straight but somewhat tilted. The Earth rotates from the west to the east. When you are in India, the north-eastern state of Arunachal Pradesh gets the first sunrise (dawn). The Earth takes 24 hours to complete one rotation. This means a complete rotation has both day and night.

During the rotation of the Earth, one half of the Earth faces the sun and the other half is away from the sun. The part that faces the sun directly has day and the part that is away from the sun has night. Day and night follow each other as the Earth rotates on its axis every 24 hours.

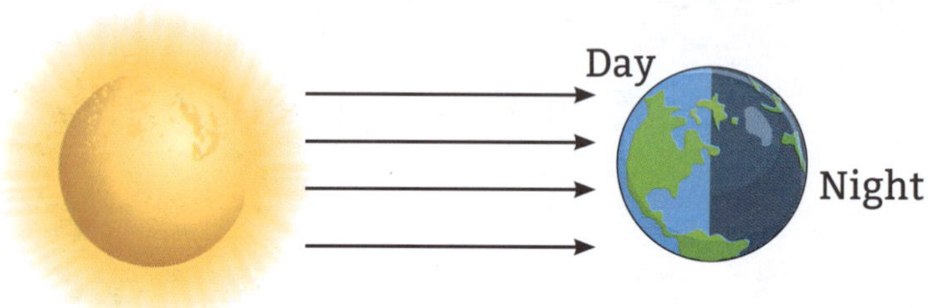

Day and night

Science in Context

Japan is the country that gets the first sunlight. Thus, it is called the 'land of the rising sun'.

Activity

Aim: To understand how rotation of the Earth causes day and night

Materials required: A globe, a table lamp, a sketch pen or marker

Procedure:

1. Place the globe in a dark room.
2. Keep the table lamp about 60 cm away from the globe.
3. Check the directions north, south, east and west on the globe.
4. Mark your favourite country as a reference point with a sketch pen.
5. Switch on the lamp. It acts as the sun. Focus the light of the lamp on the reference point. This shows daylight.
6. Slowly rotate the globe from west to east from your reference point.

Observation:

As the reference point slowly gets away from the light source, it becomes dark there, which shows night. This indicates that the rotation of the Earth on its axis causes day and night.

Revolution

Revolution is the movement of the Earth around the sun on a fixed path.

The fixed path on which the Earth goes around the sun is called the **orbit**.

The position of the Earth in its orbit around the sun determines the seasons on the Earth.

The time taken by the Earth to complete one revolution around the sun is 365¼ days, which is roughly a year for us.

Earth rotates on its axis as it revolves around the sun

The rotation and revolution of the Earth occur simultaneously.

HUMAN BEINGS AND EARTH

The Earth has air, water and land with plants, trees and animals.

Over the years, the human population has increased. With the increase in population, the number of houses, offices, hotels, industries, vehicles, etc. has also increased.

The environment getting dirty

Clean and green environment

Trees are cut down to build most of these structures. Smoke from vehicles and factories has made the air we breathe impure.

The water in the rivers and lakes has become dirty due to the waste dumped by industries and houses. All these have made our environment dirty.

We must plant more trees and dispose waste properly to keep our environment clean and green.

Go Green

Earth Day is celebrated on 22nd April every year. On this day, all over the world, adults and children learn about the planet Earth and its importance. They are made aware of the benefits we get from the Earth. We should not destroy forests, animals, birds, etc. We should keep the Earth clean and green.

Keywords

Atmosphere: The blanket of air around the Earth

Axis: It is an imaginary line passing through the centre of the Earth upon which the Earth spins

Rotation: The movement of the Earth on its own axis

Orbit: It is the path of movement of the Earth around the sun

Revolution: The movement of the Earth around the sun on a fixed path

Summary

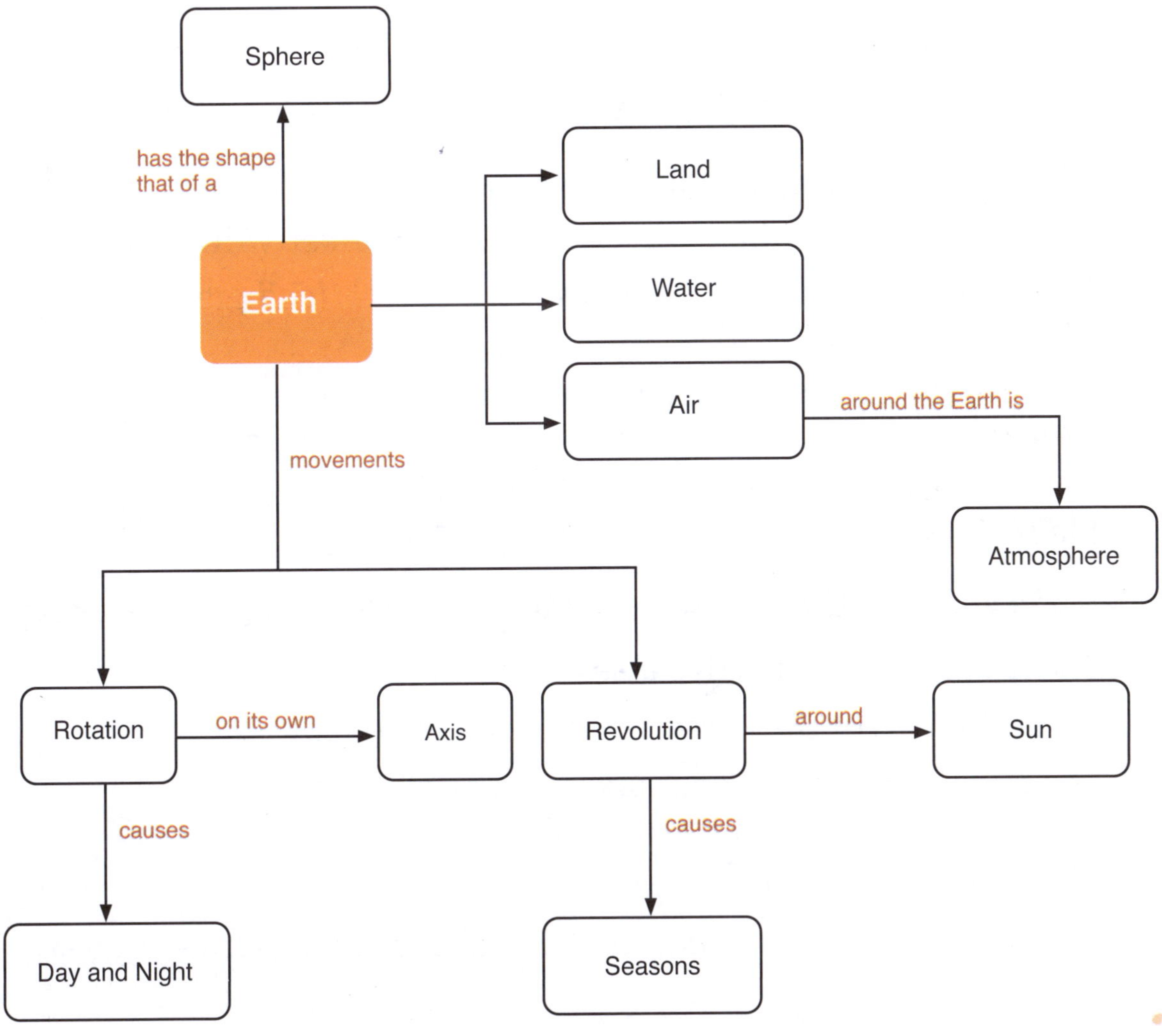

EXERCISE

W

A. Choose the correct option for each of the following. ia

1. Earlier people believed that the Earth was ____________.
   (a) square (b) flat (c) spherical (d) none
2. The axis of the Earth is ____________.
   (a) straight (b) rounded (c) tilted (d) curved
3. The light from the sun is used by ____________.
   (a) birds (b) animals (c) plants (d) all of these
4. What is the time taken by the Earth to complete one rotation?
   (a) 12 hours (b) 15 hours (c) 24 hours (d) 60 hours
5. The Earth rotates from ____________.
   (a) west to east (b) east to west (c) east to south (d) none

B. Fill in the blanks with the correct words. ia

1. ____________ covers the entire Earth like a blanket. (Air/Water)
2. When the Earth rotates, it causes ____________. (change in seasons/day and night)
3. The orbit of the Earth is a path around ____________. (the sun/its own axis)
4. One complete revolution of the Earth makes one ____________. (day/year)

C. State whether the following statements are true (T) or false (F).

1. The rotation of the Earth causes seasons. ☐
2. Three-fourths of the Earth's surface is covered by land. ☐
3. The revolution of the Earth takes 24 hours. ☐
4. As Earth rotates, the side of Earth facing away from the sun experiences daylight. ☐
5. Smoke from vehicles makes the air we breathe impure. ☐

D. Name the following.

1. Two things we get from the sun ____________ and ____________
2. Two types of movements of the Earth ____________ and ____________
3. Two things the Earth has to support life ____________ and ____________

E. Give reasons for the following.

1. The Earth looks blue from outer space.
2. Rotation of the Earth causes day and night.
3. Sun supports life on Earth.
4. Japan is called the 'Land of the rising sun'.
5. We must plant more trees and dispose waste properly.

F. Answer the following questions briefly.

1. What is atmosphere?
2. What is the axis of the Earth?
3. What are the poles of the Earth? Name them.
4. What is an orbit?

G. Answer the following questions.

1. How can you say that the Earth is spherical?
2. How do day and night occur on the Earth?
3. Explain the difference between the two movements shown by the Earth.

COGNITIVE CORNER

Critical Thinking

1. When it is day in Chennai, India, what will it be in Detroit, USA?
2. Imagine you are sailing on a ship away from the harbour. You observe a tall building in the city. When you move far in the sea, the building seems to move away from your sight. Which part of the building becomes invisible to you first?

Picture Study

Look at the following diagrams and write which movement of the Earth is being shown in each picture.

____________________ ____________________

Project

Make your own coin box using empty plastic bottles. With the help of an elder, cut a slit on the side of the bottle to insert money through it. Use a marker pen to make the eyes and nose of your coin box near the cap of the bottle. Use coloured paper to make its ears and tail.

Life Skills

We can help in keeping the Earth clean by following the rule of 3 Rs. They are—reduce, reuse and recycle. Make a chart/poster as shown alongside and write down three ways by which you can reduce, reuse and recycle items.

How can I **reduce** the things I waste?	How can I **reuse** things at school?	How can I **recycle** things at home?
__________	__________	__________
__________	__________	__________
__________	__________	__________
__________	__________	__________

WORKSHEET

What makes Earth a unique planet?

The table given below shows the factors that make life possible on the Earth.

Factors	
Temperature	Life seems limited to a specific temperature range. In this range, liquid water can still exist under certain conditions. Out of all the planets, only Earth's surface is in this temperature range.
Water	Water is regularly available.
Atmosphere	Earth has the right size to hold a sufficient-sized atmosphere. Earth's atmosphere keeps the surface warm and protects it from radiation.

We are lucky that Earth has chosen us to live on it. We should not spoil Earth's air and water.

Draw and colour a poster on 'Save Earth'.

11 Soil

Learning Checklist

- Formation of soil
- Layers of soil
- What does soil contain?
- Types of soil
- Uses of soil

Let's Get Started

Identify the terms from the given box and write the correct answer that matches each statement given below the pictures.

Clay	Soil	Sand

I am found at a beach or in the desert.

____

I am very important for the plants to grow.

____

I am used by potters to make pots and toys.

____

In this chapter, let us learn how soil is formed, what does it contain and its uses.

The Earth is a beautiful planet. There are mountains and plains, hills and valleys, deserts, seas and oceans on the Earth. Soil forms the uppermost layer of the Earth's surface on which plants grow.

FORMATION OF SOIL

It takes thousands of years for soil to form. There are huge rocks on the Earth's surface. These rocks are broken down into smaller pieces due to the heat of the sun, water from the rains and strong winds. These smaller pieces of rocks are carried away by strong wind and rainwater to distant places. The smaller pieces rub against each other and break down further to become fine particles of soil.

The slow process in which the rocks break down into smaller pieces due to the action of wind, water and the heat of the sun is called **weathering**. During this process, dead plants and animals also mix with the soil making it rich in minerals and nutrients.

Action of sun's heat on rocks

Action of rain on rocks

Dead plants and animals get mixed with the soil

Fine particles of soil

Formation of soil

Science in Context

The study of rocks and soil on Earth is called geology. A scientist who studies about the earth and its components is called a geologist.

LAYERS OF SOIL

The soil is divided into different layers. The four main layers of soil are as follows.

Topsoil

Plants use some substances present in the soil to grow well. These substances are called **nutrients**. The soil rich in nutrients is called **fertile soil**. The topmost and the most fertile layer of the soil on which plants grow is called the topsoil.

Topsoil is rich in humus. The remains of dead plants and animals mixed with the soil is called **humus**. Humus makes the soil fertile.

Subsoil

The layer below the topsoil is called the subsoil. The subsoil contains small stones and pebbles.

Parent rock

The parent rock is a layer of small weathered rocks that lies below the subsoil. These rocks have cracks in them.

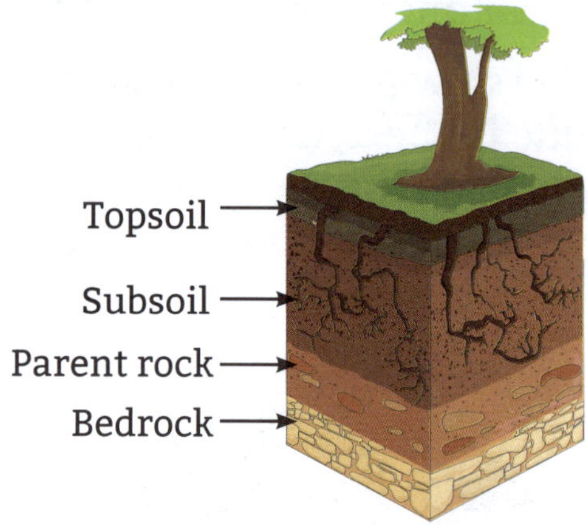

A soil profile

Bedrock

Bedrock is the last layer and contains unweathered solid hard rocks.

WHAT DOES SOIL CONTAIN?

Let us perform an activity to understand what soil is made up of.

Activity 1

Aim: To find out what soil contains

Materials required: Soil, a transparent jar and clear water

Procedure: Take a transparent jar. Put a handful of garden soil into the jar. Fill the jar with water, close the jar with a lid and shake it well. Leave it undisturbed for some time and observe what happens.

Observation:

(a) Small stones deposit at the bottom of the jar.

(b) There is a layer of sand above the layer of stones.

(c) The clay settles down above the layer of sand.

(d) The water above the layer of clay is not clear. It is muddy water.

(e) The top layer is dark and contains light, spongy particles called humus.

Conclusion: Soil is made up of stones, sand, clay, mud particles and the remains of plants and animals.

Soil Contains Water

When soil is heated on a low flame in a covered metal vessel for 10 minutes, you can see water droplets on the inner side of the lid. This shows that soil also contains water. The water present in the soil is called **moisture**. The amount of moisture varies from soil to soil.

Soil contains water

Soil Contains Air

Let us do an activity to show that soil contains air.

Activity 2

Aim: To show that soil contains air

Materials required: Soil, a transparent container and clear water

Procedure: Take some garden soil. Put the soil in a transparent container so that the container is half full. Pour water on the soil.

Observation: You will notice bubbles of air rising up from the surface of the soil.

Conclusion: This shows that there is air trapped in the soil particles which escapes out as bubbles.

Revise and Recall

Fill in the blanks using the correct words.

1. Sun's heat, rainwater and ____________ break down huge rocks into smaller pieces. (wind/humans)

2. Soil is divided into ________ main layers. (two/four)
3. The remains of dead plants and animals mixed with the soil is called ________. (humus/soil)
4. The layer below the topsoil is called ________. (bedrock/subsoil)
5. The water present in the soil is called ________. (humidity/moisture)

TYPES OF SOIL

a

There are different types of soil. Soil can be black, dark brown or red in colour.

Gravel

Gravel is made up of mainly small and big stones. As there is a lot of space between the pieces of gravel, it holds a lot of air. It does not hold any water. Gravel is mainly used in constructing buildings.

Gravel made of small and big stones

Sandy soil

Sandy soil is generally light brown in colour. It consists of small particles or grains of sand which are loosely packed. It holds a lot of air between its particles. As the sand particles are loosely packed, water drains off very quickly. Sandy soil is mostly found in deserts and near seashores. Date palms, desert plants and coconut trees grow in sandy soil.

Clayey soil

Clayey soil is made up of very fine particles which are closely packed. Therefore, it is able to hold water for a long time and is sticky. As there is no space between the clay particles, it cannot hold any air. It is used to make pots, showcase articles and playthings. Plants such as rice and wheat grow well in clayey soil.

Loam

Loam is a mixture of sand, clay and humus. It can hold some amount of air as well as water. The soil is also rich in minerals. It is suitable to grow fruits and vegetables.

Sandy soil

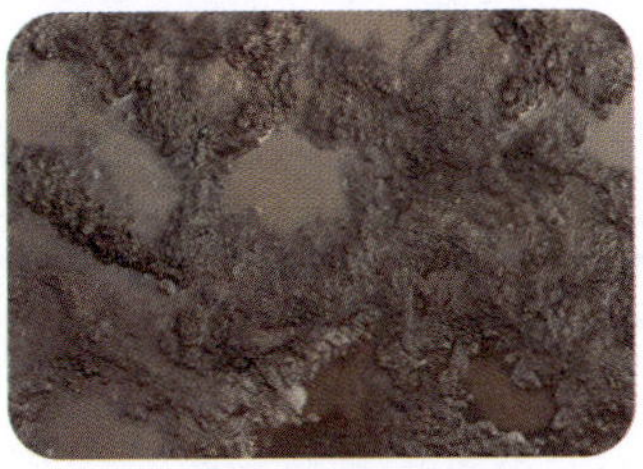

Clayey soil

Loam

USES OF SOIL

Soil is useful for both plant and animal life. Roots hold the plants firmly with the help of the soil.

Farmers grow various crops and plants in the soil. Plants absorb water and nutrients from the soil to grow and live.

Science in Context

Cutting down of naturally grown trees in large numbers is called **deforestation**. This leads to **soil erosion**, wherein the top fertile layer of soil is removed by wind and water.

Protecting soil from erosion is called **soil conservation**.

Soil is also a home for many insects and small animals. Insects such as ants, grasshoppers and crickets live in the soil. Earthworms, centipedes, scorpions and millipedes make burrows in the soil. The waste of these animals makes the soil fertile. Small animals such as rats, moles and rabbits build their homes in the soil. They dig deep burrows in the soil which help water and air to mix well with the soil.

Ants, scorpions, earthworms and rabbits live in soil

Keywords

Weathering: The slow process in which the rocks break down into smaller pieces due to the action of wind, water and the heat of the sun

Fertile soil: The soil rich in nutrients

Topsoil: The topmost and the most fertile layer of the soil on which plants grow

Humus: The remains of dead plants and animals mixed with the soil

Summary

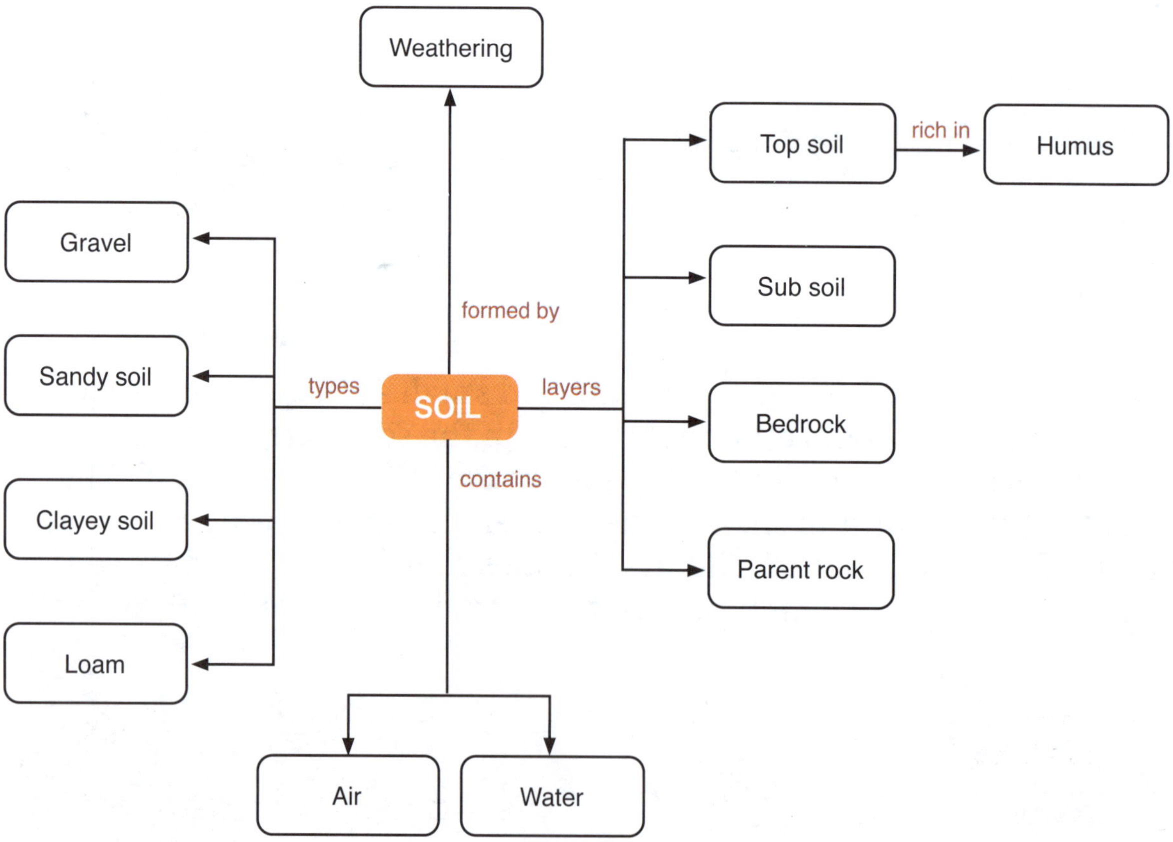

EXERCISE

W

A. Choose the correct option for each of the following.

ia

1. The soil rich in nutrients is called ____________.
   (a) clay (b) fertile soil (c) gravel (d) sand
2. ____________ is the uppermost layer of the Earth's surface.
   (a) Air (b) Soil (c) Sun (d) None
3. We find this type of soil in deserts and near seashores.
   (a) Sand (b) Loam (c) Clay (d) Gravel
4. ____________ is a mixture of sand, clay and humus.
   (a) Gravel (b) Clay (c) Loam (d) Sand
5. Which of the following does not live in soil?
   (a) Rabbit (b) Rat
   (c) Parrot (d) Earthworm

B. Fill in the blanks with the correct words.

ia

1. __________ break down to form stones, pebbles and soil. (Rocks/Sand)
2. __________ is formed by the breaking down of rocks. (River/Soil)
3. __________ are the substances which make the soil fertile. (Rocks/Nutrients)
4. ____________ is used in construction of buildings. (Gravel/Loam)
5. __________ is the best soil for growing fruits and vegetables. (Sand/Loam)

C. Match the following.

ia

	Column A		Column B
1.	Bedrock	(a)	Soil rich in nutrients
2.	Fertile soil	(b)	Live inside the soil
3.	Clayey soil	(c)	Non-porous layer
4.	Centipedes and scorpions	(d)	Cannot hold air

D. **Give two examples for each of the following.**

1. Layers of soil ________ and ________
2. Kinds of soil ________ and ________
3. Plants that grow in sandy soil ________ and ________
4. Insects that live in soil ________ and ________
5. Animals that build their homes in soil ________ and ________

E. **Give reasons for the following.**

1. Topsoil is the most fertile layer of the soil.
2. When soil is heated on a low flame in a covered metal vessel for 5-10 minutes, you can see water droplets on the inner side of the lid.
3. Soil is useful for both plant and animal life.
4. Gravel soil holds a lot of air but it does not hold any water.
5. Clayey soil cannot hold air.

F. **Answer the following questions briefly.**

1. What is soil? What does it contain?
2. Name the different layers of soil.
3. What is loam?
4. Write any two uses of soil.

G. **Answer the following questions.**

1. How is soil formed?
2. Explain the different layers of soil with the help of a diagram.
3. How can you prove that soil contains air?
4. Name the different types of soil. Also, give one use of each type.

COGNITIVE CORNER

Critical Thinking

1. How do the insects and animals that live in the soil help in making it fertile?
2. Have you observed trees falling down after heavy rains? Why does it happen?

Picture Study

Which soil is used for the following activities? Write the name in the space provided below.

Constructing a building

____

Growing fruits and vegetables

____

Making pots and articles

____

Project

Draw the process of soil formation on a chart paper. Display the chart in your class and speak about each stage.

Life Skills

Look at the picture given below. Is this the right way to treat soil? Discuss.

WORKSHEET

Nature recycles leaves and plants. In a forest, leaves fall and spread around or over a plant to enrich the soil. Over the time, they decompose into nutrients.

Compost is a nutrient-rich soil that is created when natural materials such as leaves, grass clippings, fruit peels, etc. are decomposed naturally.

You can recycle leaves and other plant materials at home by setting up a compost bin.

Compostable household materials include eggshells (not eggs), used coffee, tea leaves, leaves, twigs, branches, newspapers, hair, fruit and vegetable peels. Materials that should not get composted are the ones that do not break down easily, such as meat, cheese, milk, oils and bones.

Set up your own compost bin!

Which of the following materials can be added to the compost?

Metals ☐ Glass ☐ Eggs ☐ Cardboard ☐

12 Solids, Liquids and Gases

Learning Checklist

- Solids, liquids and gases
- Change of forms

Let's Get Started

You have learned in earlier classes that water exists in three different forms. Look at the pictures given below and answer the questions. (Hint: All answers are forms of water.)

What is coming out of the mouth of the kettle?

____

What is the boy drinking?

____

What is the girl putting in the glass?

____

Like water, different things exist in different forms, that is, as solids, liquids or gases. Some things exist in solid form, some in liquid form and some in gaseous form.

But how do we know if something is solid, liquid or gas?

SOLIDS

Look at the picture given alongside. Do these stones occupy space? Yes, they occupy space. Even if we keep the stones inside a bowl, their shape will not change.

Stones inside a jar

Things that have a fixed shape and size and occupy a fixed space are called **solids**. Things such as pencils, books and erasers are examples of solids.

Solid things do not move or flow by themselves. Hence, they cannot be poured into containers.

Pencil

Book

LIQUIDS

Look at the picture given alongside. Water has been kept in three different containers.

Is the shape of the water similar to the shape of the container? Yes, water takes the shape of the container it is poured into.

Water in three containers

Things that do not have a fixed shape and take the shape of the container they are poured into are called **liquids**. Things such as milk, honey and water are examples of liquids.

Milk

Honey

Liquids occupy space. When we pour water into a jar, it occupies the space in the jar.

Pour a mug of water on the floor. Does the water flow by itself? Yes, it does. So, liquids flow by themselves.

GASES

Football filled with air

Water vapour

Air is all around us. It does not have a fixed shape. Air is actually a mixture of gases such as oxygen and carbon dioxide. Things that do not have a fixed shape or size and do not occupy a fixed space are called **gases**. Air and water vapour are common examples of **gases**.

Take a needle and prick a balloon filled with air. Where did the air inside the balloon go? Gases flow in all directions very easily.

Revise and Recall

Identify the following things as solid, liquid or gas.

____

____

____

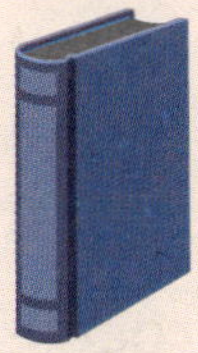

____

____

CHANGE OF FORMS

a

The different forms of water can be changed from one form to another by heating or cooling.

The process in which a solid turns into liquid on heating is called **melting**.

The process in which a liquid turns into solid on cooling is called **freezing**.

The process in which a liquid turns into gas on heating is called **evaporation**.

Science in Context

Water is the only liquid that can exist in all three forms, ice, water and water vapour.

The process in which a gas turns into liquid on cooling is called **condensation**.

The above processes indicate that heating or cooling can change the forms of water. Water evaporates to form water vapour. Water vapour condenses to form water. You must have seen droplets of water on the outer surface of cold drink bottles. These droplets are formed when water vapour in the air condenses to form water.

Water freezes to form ice and ice melts to form water.

Snowman Melted snow (water) Vapour

Keywords

Solid: Things that have a fixed shape and size and occupy a fixed space

Liquid: Things that have no fixed shape but occupy a fixed space

Gas: Things that have no fixed shape and do not occupy a fixed space

Melting: The process in which a solid turns into liquid on heating

Freezing: The process in which a liquid turns into solid on cooling

Evaporation: The process in which a liquid turns into gas on heating

Condensation: The process in which a gas turns into liquid on cooling

Summary

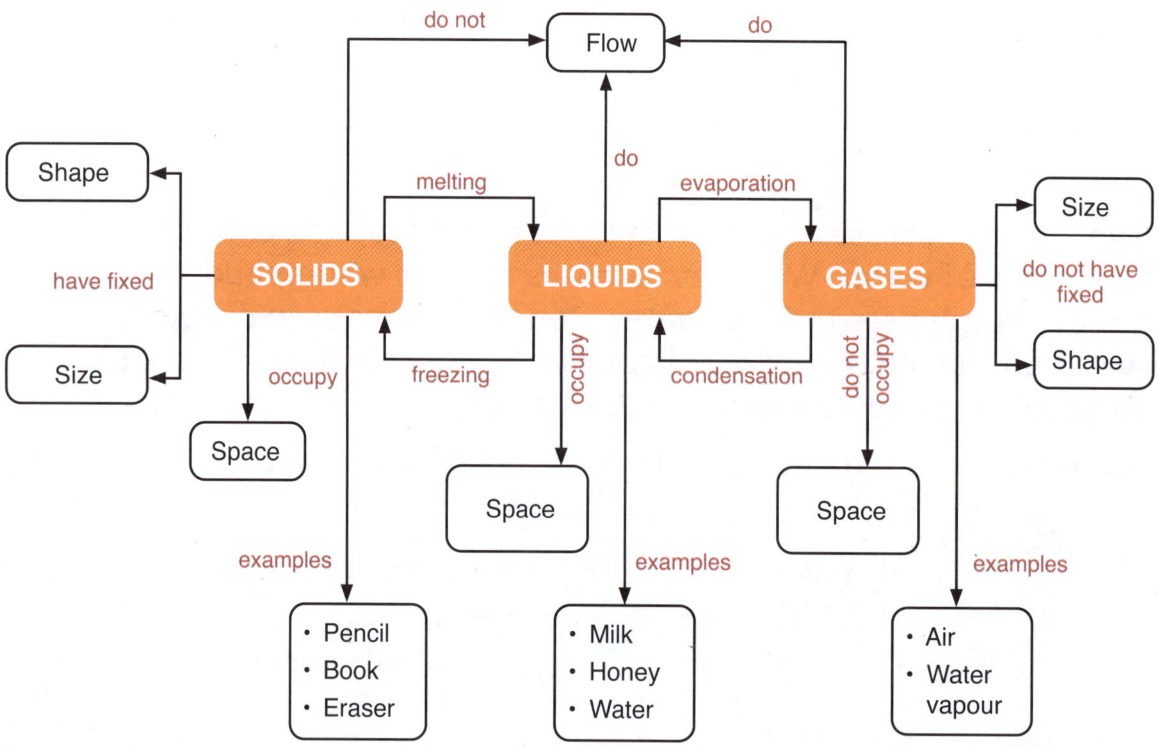

EXERCISE

W

ia

A. Fill in the blanks with the correct words.

1. ______________ have a fixed shape. (Solids/Liquids)
2. ______________ occupy a fixed space. (Liquids/Gases)
3. ______________ is an example of liquid. (Milk/Pencil)
4. Air is an example of ______________. (solid/gas)
5. Ice is the ______________ form of water. (solid/liquid)

B. State whether the following statements are true (T) or false (F).

ia

1. Solids do not occupy any space. ☐
2. Liquid turns into gas on cooling. ☐
3. Gases do not flow by themselves. ☐
4. Water exists in all the three forms. ☐
5. Honey is an example of solid. ☐

C. Match the following.

ia

	Column A		Column B
1.	Oxygen	(a)	Liquid
2.	Pencil	(b)	Gas
3.	Milk	(c)	Solid

D. Give two examples for each of the following.

1. Solids ______________________ and ______________________
2. Liquids ______________________ and ______________________
3. Gases ______________________ and ______________________

E. Give reasons for the following.

1. If we keep a solid object inside a bowl, its shape will not change.
2. Heating or cooling can change the forms of water.
3. Gases flow easily by themselves.
4. Milk flows when poured down.

F. Answer the following questions briefly.

1. Write two properties of solids.
2. Write two properties of liquids.
3. Write two properties of gases.
4. How does a block of ice change into water?

G. Answer the following questions.

1. What are the differences between solids, liquids and gases?
2. What is the difference between melting and freezing?
3. How is evaporation different from condensation?
4. How does water change its forms? Explain.

COGNITIVE CORNER

Critical Thinking

1. A perfume sprayed on one end of a room makes the whole room smell good. Why?
2. Your mom has packed hot *idlies* for lunch. When you open your lunch box at school, you see droplets of water on the inner side of the lid sometimes. Can you explain why?

Picture Study

Look at the pictures. Fill in the blanks.

_________ + _________ = _________

This process is known as _________ .

Project

Collect pictures of any six things found at your home. Paste these in your scrapbook and write whether it is solid, liquid or gas below each picture.

Life Skills

Name the process that is responsible for each daily-life instance given below.

(a) Water droplets gather on the mirror during a hot bath. _________

(b) Wet clothes dry when put out in the sun. _________

9 INDUSTRY, INNOVATION AND INFRASTRUCTURE

WORKSHEET

Design a Toy Using Solid, Liquid and Gas

You have the following materials:

Solids:

- Cardboard, cards, papers
- String, yarn, wiggly eyes
- Thermocol
- Paper clips
- Any other thing of your choice!

Liquids:

- Paints
- Glue
- Water (inside balloon)
- Glitter bottles
- Any other thing of your choice!

Gases:

- Sponges
- Balloons
- Bubble wrap
- Small balls

13 Light, Sound and Force

Learning Checklist

- Luminous and non-luminous objects
- Shadow
- Sound
- Force

Let's Get Started

Look at the image given below carefully and colour the objects that give out light.

Will you be able to see things kept inside a dark room? No. To see things kept inside a dark room, you require a source of light. The light from the source falls on the objects and helps us to see them.

LUMINOUS AND NON-LUMINOUS OBJECTS

Objects that give out light are called **luminous objects**. Some examples of luminous objects are given below.

Sun

Bulb

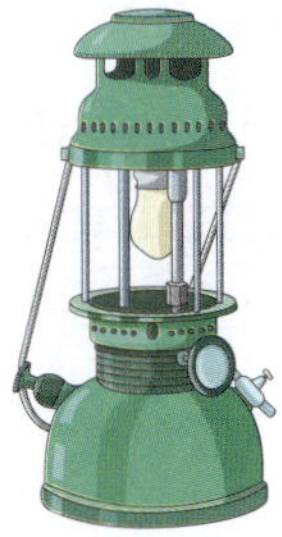

Lantern

Objects that do not give out light are called **non-luminous objects**. We can see non-luminous objects only when light falls on them.

Some examples of non-luminous objects are given below.

Table

Books

Science in Context

It is highly dangerous to look at the sun directly through the naked eyes. One can use sunglasses to look at the sun.

SHADOW

a

You might have noticed that when light falls on an object, a dark patch is formed on the opposite side of the source of light. This dark patch is called a **shadow**.

So, we can say that a shadow is formed when an object stands in the path of light. As a result, the object blocks the path of the light coming from a light source. During the day, we get to see shadows when objects block the light coming from the sun.

Shadow of a boy

At night, shadows are formed when objects block the light coming from an artificial light source such as bulb, candle, etc.

For shadows to form, a light source, an object and a screen are required. The size of the shadow of an object depends on the position of the light source, the object and the screen.

Shadows of objects formed with the help of sunlight are longer during the morning and evening, and the shortest at noon.

Activity

Aim: To understand the change in the length of the shadow of a stick under the sun during daytime

Materials required:

- Stick of length 30 cm
- Metre ruler

Procedure:

- Place the stick upright in an open ground during the morning time on a clear sunny day.
- Measure the length of the shadow formed in the morning.

Shadow on the ground

- Measure the length of the shadow again at noon.
- Repeat the same in the evening before leaving the school.

Observation:

Length of the shadow during morning	
Length of the shadow at noon	
Length of the shadow during evening	

Conclusion: The size of the shadow is the longest during the morning and evening, and the shortest at noon.

Features of a Shadow

Following are the features of a shadow:

- A shadow cannot be formed in the absence of a light source.
- A shadow is always dark, irrespective of the colour of the object.

- The size of the shadow varies according to the position of the source of light.

SOUND

Every day we get to hear various sounds such as people speaking, bells ringing, birds chirping and so on. Some sounds are loud (e.g., shouting) and some are soft (e.g., whispering). Some sounds are pleasant while others are unpleasant. The sound of the traffic will be unpleasant to your ears. On the other hand, you would not mind sitting through a musical show for a long time.

Sounds that are good and pleasant to your ears are called **music**, and sounds that disturb you and are not good or pleasant to your ears are called **noise**.

Music: Singer performing

Noise: Cars honking

Revise and Recall

Fill in the blanks with the correct words.

1. Sun is a ____________ object. (luminous/non-luminous)
2. A shadow is formed on the ___________ side of the source of light with respect to object. (opposite/same)
3. Sounds that disturb you and are not good or pleasant to your ears are called ___________(noise/music)
4. A shadow of an object is always ________ (bright/dark)
5. Shadows of objects formed with the help of sunlight are the __________ at noon. (longest/shortest)

FORCE

All the actions that we do in our daily lives to move an object can be broadly grouped as a **push** or a **pull**.

A push

A pull

A push or a pull applied on an object is called **force**.

If a body moves due to the action of a push or a pull, we can say that force has been applied on the body.

Effects of Force

Force has various effects on the objects on which it is applied. Some effects are given below.

- Force can make an object move.
- Force can make a moving object stop.
- Force can change the shape of an object.
- Force can change the direction of a moving object.

Force makes a ball move

Force stops a moving ball

Force changes the shape of an object

Friction

Friction is a force that slows down the movement of an object. Thus, in order to move an object, the force applied through a push or pull should be greater than the force of friction.

> **Science in Context**
>
> What we see may not be true always. A smooth granite surface offers more friction than a rough surface filled with sand.

If there is too much friction, objects do not move and if there is very less friction, objects would slide. You will find it difficult to walk on a wet surface because there is less frictional force.

Keywords

Luminous objects: Objects that give out light

Non-luminous objects: Objects that do not give out light

Shadow: A dark patch formed when the path of light is blocked by an object

Music: Sounds that are pleasant to ears

Noise: Sounds that are unpleasant to ears

Force: A push or a pull applied on an object

Friction: A force that slows down the movement of an object

Summary

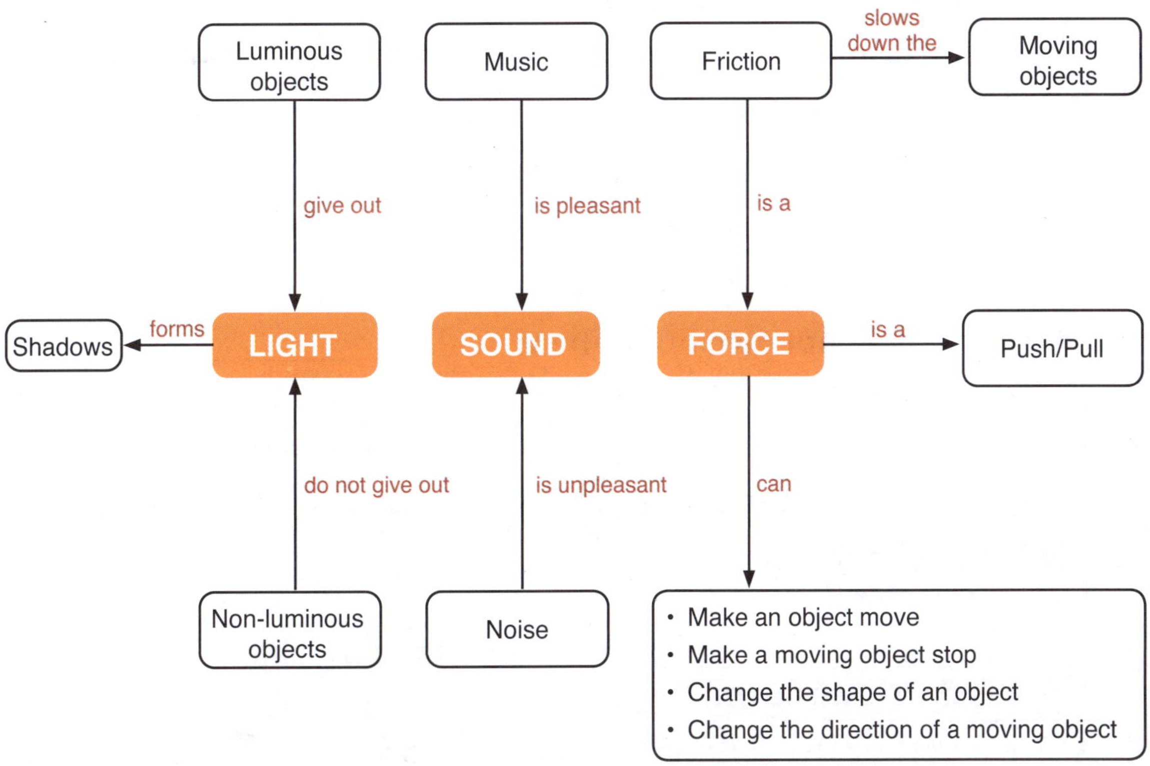

EXERCISE

W

A. Choose the correct option for each of the following. ia

1. We see objects when __________ .
   (a) light falls on the objects (b) objects produce own light
   (c) our eyes produce light (d) light falls on us
2. Shadow can be formed only if there is/are ______________ .
   (a) object (b) light
   (c) screen (d) object, light and screen
3. The longest shadow of an object under the sun is formed during _________ .
   (a) morning (b) evening
   (c) noon (d) morning and evening
4. Which of the following sounds would be called music?
   (a) A child crying (b) An artist playing a flute
   (c) School bell ringing (d) Car horn
5. A push or a pull applied on an object is called ____________ .
   (a) motion (b) sound (c) light (d) force

B. Fill in the blanks with the correct words. ia

1. Objects that do not give out light are called ________________ objects. (luminous/non-luminous)
2. Music is a/an ________________ sound. (pleasant/unpleasant)
3. ________________ can make an object move. (Force/Friction)
4. Force can change the ________________ of an object. (shape/colour)
5. Friction ________________ the movement of an object. (speeds up/slows down)

C. State whether the following statements are true (T) or false (F). ia

1. A shadow is always dark, irrespective of the colour of the object. ☐
2. Noise is pleasant to your ears. ☐

3. To move a table, you need to push or pull it. ☐
4. Force can make a moving object stop. ☐
5. If there is too much friction, objects would slide. ☐

D. Give two examples for each of the following.

1. Luminous objects ____________ and ____________
2. Non-luminous objects ____________ and ____________
3. Pleasant sounds ____________ and ____________
4. Unpleasant sounds ____________ and ____________
5. Effects of force ____________ and ____________

E. Give reasons for the following.

1. A bulb is a luminous object.
2. A table is a non-luminous object.
3. A shadow cannot be formed in the absence of a light source.
4. The sound of traffic is considered as noise.
5. We will find it difficult to walk on a wet surface.

F. Answer the following questions briefly.

1. What helps us to see objects around us?
2. Name the three things required to form a shadow.
3. Write any two features of a shadow.
4. What are the different types of sounds we hear?
5. What is friction?

G. Answer the following questions.

1. What is the difference between luminous and non-luminous objects? Give one example of each.
2. What is a shadow? Explain how it is formed.
3. Distinguish between pleasant and unpleasant sounds with examples.
4. Explain the effects of force with an example.

COGNITIVE CORNER

Critical Thinking

1. Why do we slip when we step on a banana peel?
2. Write yes or no.

(a) Can a smaller light source, a larger object and a screen form a shadow? ☐

(b) Can a larger light source, a smaller object and a screen form a shadow? ☐

Picture Study

Match the following.

1. 

2. 

3. 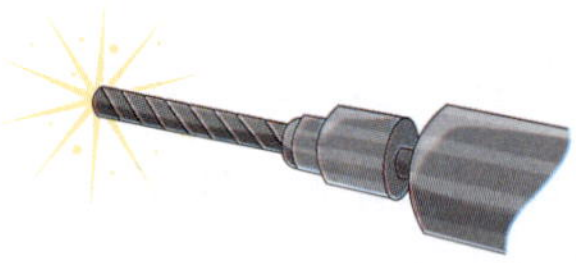

4. 

(a) Luminous object (b) Non-luminous object (c) Music (d) Noise

Project

Draw a rough sketch of your study room with all the objects that may help you to study. Consider the following: (a) Sufficient lighting (b) Less noise

Life Skills

If someone is driving a car and gets stuck in a traffic jam, how should he/she behave? Select from the options given below.

(a) Keep honking your car horn. ☐

(b) Stop your vehicle and play the music loudly. ☐

(c) Relax and wait for the traffic police to clear the jam. ☐

WORKSHEET

Unpleasant sounds are called noise. Noise is uncomfortable to our ears. Loud noise is harmful for the ears. It can permanently damage our ears and cause loss of hearing.

Some people have to work in places where the level of loud noise is very high. They have to listen to the noise for long hours. This can even lead to loss of hearing. Here are some examples of such jobs.

Construction worker

Traffic police

Steel cutter

To prevent hearing loss, these workers should wear protective equipments such as earplugs or earmuffs when needed.

You can help people by doing things that reduce noise pollution.

Draw a poster on how to reduce noise pollution.

14 Measurement

Learning Checklist

- Measurement of length
- Measurement of mass
- Measurement of capacity
- Measurement of time

Let's Get Started

Look at the pictures given below and answer the questions that follow.

Which pencil is longer? ________ Which bottle will hold more water? ________

In our everyday life, we often come across situations where we need to find the length, weight, height or amount of different objects.

Finding out the size or quantity of an object is called **measurement**.

MEASUREMENT OF LENGTH

Do you have a ruler in your pencil box? What do you use it for? Look at the pictures of books given alongside. Take a ruler and measure the length of the books. Which one is longer?

Length tells us how long an object is. In earlier times, people used to measure length using their body parts.

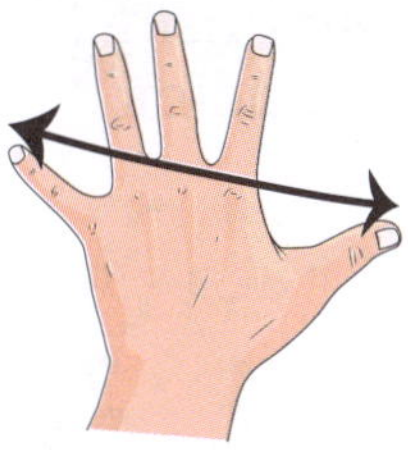

Hand span

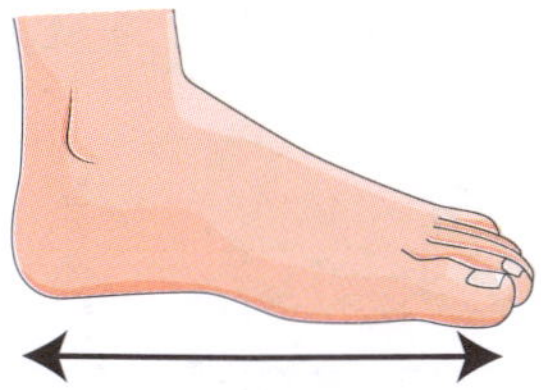

Foot

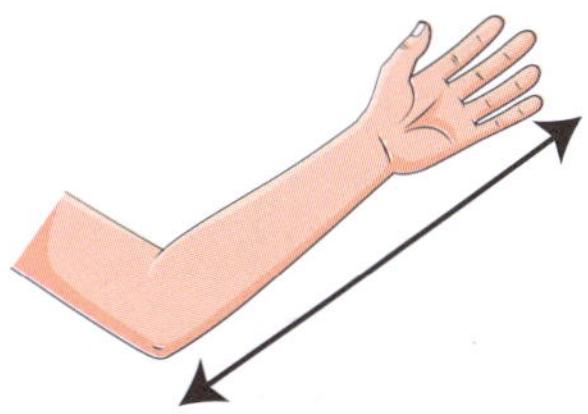

Cubit

Pace

However, measurements using body parts are not very accurate. This is because body parts of two different people will have different sizes. For example, if you measure the length of your desk using hand span and then your teacher does the same, both of you will have different results.

Therefore, we should have fixed standards of measurement to avoid confusion.

Fixed standards of measurements are called **units**. Units used for measuring length are kilometre (km), metre (m) and centimetre (cm).

Length can be measured by using a measuring tape and a ruler.

MEASUREMENT OF MASS

Beam balance

Digital balance

Place one notebook on your right hand and two notebooks of the same weight on your left hand. Which hand feels heavier?

Measuring mass helps us to find out how heavy or light an object is. Mass is commonly measured in units such as kilogram (kg) and gram (g). Mass can be measured by using a beam balance, a spring balance and a digital balance.

MEASUREMENT OF CAPACITY

The amount of liquid a container can hold is called its **capacity**.

Capacity is commonly measured in units such as litre (ℓ) and millilitre (mℓ) for liquids.

Measuring jars and measuring cylinders are commonly used to measure liquids.

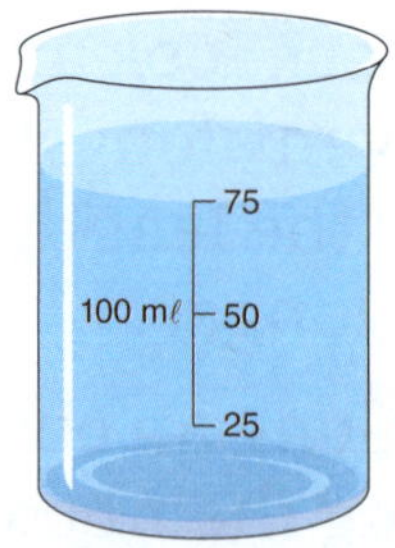

Measuring jar (beaker)

Measuring cylinders

Activity

Aim: To calculate the capacity of a vessel using a measuring jar

Materials required:

- A jug
- A bowl of water
- A measuring jar—100 mℓ

Procedure:

1. Take an empty jug and place it on a table. We need to find the capacity of the jug.
2. Fill a measuring jar with water from the bowl.
3. Pour water from the measuring jar into the jug. Note down the amount of water poured into the jug in the observation table.
4. Repeat Step 3 till the jug gets completely filled with water. In the final count, use only the amount of water required to fill the jug. Note the measurements accordingly.
5. Finally, add the amount of water poured each time.

Observation:

S. No.	Amount of water poured in mℓ (millilitre)
1	
2	
3	
Total	

Conclusion: The sum total of the amount of water poured into the jug will give us the capacity of the jug.

MEASUREMENT OF TIME

How do you know when you have to get up or when is the time to go to school? You look at a clock or a watch to find out the time.

Time measurement is important in our daily lives as it helps in organizing the day-to-day events of our life. For example, waking up in the morning, going to school, having food, playing, sleeping, etc.

Time is commonly measured in units such as year, month, hour (h), minute (min) and second (sec). Sixty seconds make one minute and sixty minutes make an hour. Some of the commonly used time-measuring devices are a stopwatch, a wall clock and a wristwatch. A clock has two hands to show time. The long hand shows the minutes and the short hand shows the hours. We get information on days, months and years from a calendar.

Wall clock

Wristwatch

Science in Context

Events that are regularly repeated such as the movement of the sun, moon and stars helped our ancestors to measure time. This also helped them to construct time-measuring devices.

Revise and Recall

Fill in the blanks with the correct words.

1. _________ tells us how long an object is. (Length/Mass)
2. Fixed standards of measurements are called _______. (units/values)
3. Unit of mass is _________. (kilometre/kilogram)
4. Capacity is commonly measured in units of __________. (litre/metre)
5. Mass can be measured by using a _________. (measuring tape/beam balance)

Keywords

Measurement: Finding out the size or quantity of an object

Unit: Fixed standards of measurement

Length: Measure of how long an object is

Mass: Measure of how heavy or light an object is

Capacity: The amount of liquid a container can hold

Summary

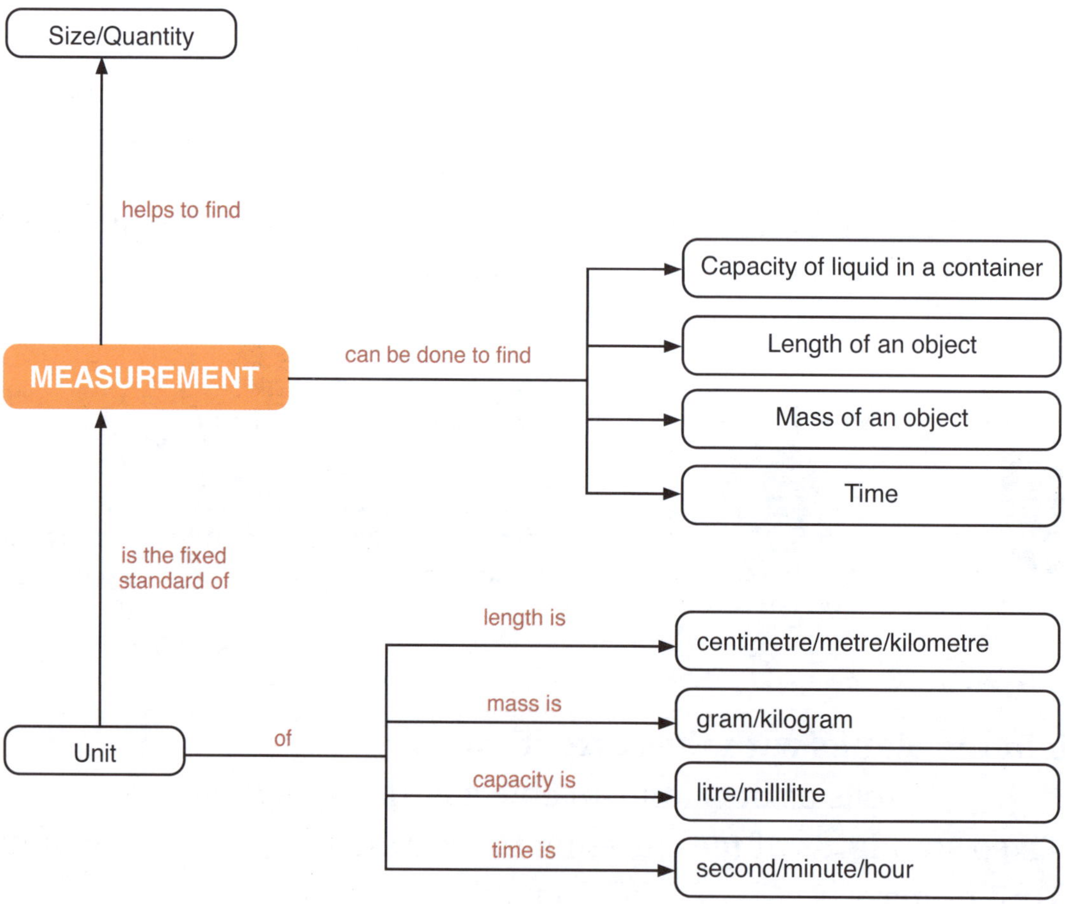

EXERCISE

W

A. Choose the correct option for each of the following. ia

1. Which of the following units is used for measuring length?
   (a) Litre (b) Metre (c) Kilogram (d) Second
2. Which of the following units is used for measuring mass?
   (a) Millilitre (b) Metre (c) Kilogram (d) Second
3. Which of the following units is used for measuring capacity?
   (a) Litre (b) Metre (c) Kilogram (d) Second
4. Which of the following units is used for measuring time?
   (a) Litre (b) Metre (c) Kilogram (d) Second
5. Which of the following devices help to measure time?
   (a) Wristwatch (b) Beam balance
   (c) Ruler (d) Measuring jar

B. Fill in the blanks with the correct words. ia

1. Use of ____________ is an inaccurate method of measuring length. (body parts/ruler)
2. Mass is measured by a ________________ . (scale/digital balance)
3. Capacity of containers is measured using the unit ________________ . (kilogram/litre)
4. Measurement of _______________ helps in organizing our day-to-day activities. (mass/time)
5. We get information on days, months and years from a ______________ . (calendar/wall clock)

C. State whether the following statements are true (T) or false (F). ia

1. Measuring tape is used for measuring length. ☐
2. Mass defines how long an object is. ☐
3. Capacity gives information on how heavy an object is. ☐
4. A wall clock shows time in minutes and hours. ☐

D. Give one example for each of the following.

1. A device used for measuring length ____________________
2. A device used for measuring mass ____________________
3. A unit used for measuring liquid capacity ________________
4. A device which can measure time in hours ________________
5. A device which can measure time in months ______________

E. Give reasons for the following.

1. Handspan is not a fixed standard unit of length.
2. Time measurement is important in our daily life.
3. We should have fixed standards of measurement.
4. Beam balance is different from a measuring cylinder.

F. Answer the following questions briefly.

1. How did people measure length in olden days?
2. Define mass. Name the units used for measuring mass.
3. What is capacity of an object? How is it measured?
4. What do the two hands of a clock show?
5. Which unit should we use to measure the following?
   (a) A tub of water
   (b) The length of a dress
   (c) To weigh tomatoes

G. Answer the following questions.

1. What is measurement? Why should we not use body parts to measure length?
2. How does time measurement help us in our daily life? Name any two time-measuring devices.

COGNITIVE CORNER

Critical Thinking

1. Sunil has a 15 cm ruler. He uses the ruler five times to measure his desk. What is the length of his desk?
2. A vegetable vendor has one 100 g, two 200 g and one 500 g stones with him. When your mother asks him to give her 800 g of onions, which stones would he use?
3. Rita has a 500 mℓ glass of water and pours the water into a jug which already has 500 mℓ of water. How much water is there in the jug?

Picture Study

Match the quantity with appropriate measuring device.

 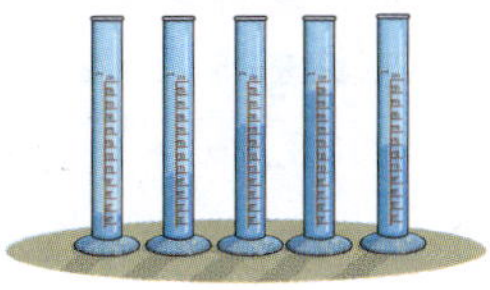  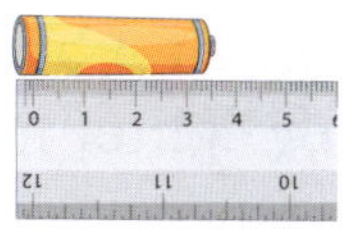

Length Mass Capacity Time

Project

Make your own weighing balance. Use the following things to make it.

(a) A plastic hanger

(b) Two paper cups

(c) Thread

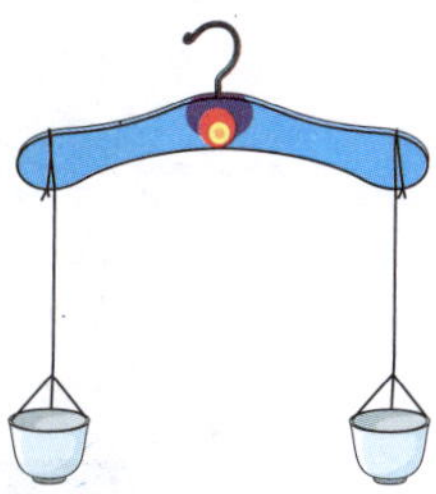

Life Skills

Find out the following information from your house.

(a) Number of tomatoes used in a week

(b) Amount of milk bought per day

(c) Capacity of your water tank

WORKSHEET

When we buy groceries from the market, we usually pay for them by mass. The method of weighing the potatoes depends on the person selling them. He can either use a beam balance or he might use a digital balance.

Beam balance

Digital scale

However long ago, when men had just started buying and selling things, they used things that were available to them to weigh things. They started using seeds and stones for buying and selling within their villages. Grains and seeds were used for lighter masses and stones for heavier ones.

It was only when trading started between different countries, that there was a need for a common measure of mass. The stone used in different places was standardized so that all the stones weighed the same. In England the 'stone' is still used as a measure of mass!

The remains of the most ancient weighing scales have been discovered in the Indus River Valley that are about four thousand years old. They looked very much like the balance beam we still use today.

Let us have fun today and see how much these objects weigh.

The lemon slices weigh ________ g.

The oranges weigh ________ kg.